ARCHAIC GREECE

ART OF THE WORLD

A SERIES OF REGIONAL HISTORIES
OF THE VISUAL ARTS

I. INDIA by Hermann Goetz

II. INDONESIA by Frits A. Wagner

III. AFRICA by Elsy Leuzinger

IV. CHINA by Werner Speiser

V. THE STONE AGE by H.-G. Bandi and others

VI. ANCIENT AMERICA by H.-D. Disselhoff and S. Linné

VII. MESOPOTAMIA AND THE MIDDLE EAST by Leonard Woolley

VIII. OCEANIA AND AUSTRALIA by Alfred Bühler, Terry Barrow and Charles P. Mountford

IX. INDOCHINA by B. Ph. Groslier

X. CRETE AND EARLY GREECE by F. Matz

XI. ROME AND HER EMPIRE by H. Kähler

XII. EGYPT by Irmgard Woldering

XIII. BURMA-KOREA-TIBET by A. B. Griswold, Chewon Kim and Peter H. Pott

XIV. THE ART OF BUDDHISM by Dietrich Seckel

XV. HIGH GOTHIC ART by Marcel Aubert

XVI. ANCIENT IRAN by Edith Porada

XVII. ETRURIA AND EARLY ROME by Guido Mansuelli

XVIII. BYZANTIUM by André Grabar

XIX. JAPAN by Peter C. Swann

XX. HELLENISTIC ART by T. B. L. Webster

XXI. ART OF THE STEPPES by K. Jettmar

XXII. CHINESE LANDSCAPE PAINTING by Anil de Silva

XXIII. CLASSICAL GREECE by Karl Schefold

XXIV. NORTH AMERICA by Wolfgang Haberland

XXV. ARCHAIC GREECE by E. Homann-Wedeking

ARCHAIC GREECE

by

E. HOMANN-WEDEKING

Translated by J. R. FOSTER

METHUEN – LONDON

Front of slip-case: Achilles binding up the wounds of Patroklos. From the inside of a bowl by the potter Sosias. About 500 B.C. *Berlin, Stiftung Preussischer Kulturbesitz, Antikensammlung. Cf. p. 188.*

Title-page: Protocorinthian vase (detail), formerly in the Chigi Collection. Third quarter of 7th century B.C. *Height of vase 10 in. Rome, Villa Giulia. Cf. pp. 56, 58.*

IN MEMORIAM
HUMFRY PAYNE

CONTENTS

List of colour plates (9). List of figures (9). Acknowledgments (10).

I. INTELLECTUAL FOUNDATIONS: THE GEOMETRIC AGE
(circa 1050–700 B.C.) 11–34

Ceramics (11). *Themes of the pictures* (14). *Ionia and Athens* (14). Small-scale sculpture (15). *Foreign influences* (17). *Religious and sociological background* (21). *Argos, Corinth and Sparta* (23). *Attica* (23). *Artistic regions* (24). Armour (28). Architecture (29). *Cult of Hera and temples of Hera* (29).

II. REVOLUTION AND CONSOLIDATION: THE ORIENTAL-IZING AGE (circa 700–620 B.C.). 35–80

Break-up of Geometric art forms. Political background. Foreign influences (35). *Crete. Cyclades. Corinth, East Greece and Athens* (36). Ceramics (37). *Relationship between small-scale and large-scale sculpture* (42). *Technical innovations* (45). *Tyranny* (47). *Relationship between sculpture and architecture* (50). Large-scale sculpture (53). *Rhodes, Corinth* (55). Ivory carving (58). Sculpture in stone, wood and bronze (61). *The kouros type* (61). *Nudity and clothing* (66). *Daidalos* (71). *Signature of artists* (72). Architecture (74). *Relationship of art to politics* (79).

III. RIPE ARCHAIC: EARLY PERIOD (circa 620–550 B.C.) 81–129

Animal figures (81). *Mythological pictures* (85). *Narrative pictures. 'Monumentalization' of Corinthian art forms* (87). *Attic influence. Solon. Nature and effect of Solonian reforms* (88). *Attic art at the beginning of the 6th century* (91). *Samian sculpture.* Geneleos (93). Ionian and Attic korai (95). *Attic sculpture in the time of Peisistratos* (99). Peisistratos (103). *Attic grave stelai* (103). *Lakonian vase-painting* (105). *Attic vase-painting.* Kleitias (107). *Painters and potters* (115). *Spatiality and the shaping of space* (116). *Temple of Hera at Olympia* (117). *Temple of Artemis at Ephesos* (118). *Temple of Apollo at Corinth* (119). *Architecture and architectural reliefs in Magna Graecia* (122). *Types of capital* (124).

7

IV. RIPE ARCHAIC: LATE PERIOD (circa 550–490 B.C.). 130–196

Art in the time of Peisistratos. Sculpture (130). Reliefs (133). *Forms of writing* (136). *Inscription and ornament* (136). Miniature art. *Bronze-casting* (137). Large bronzes (144). Vase-painting (147). *Lydos, Exekias* (147). *Amasis* (152). *Chalcidian vases* (158). *Ionian 'Little Masters'. Fikellura vases* (160). *Exekias' middle period* (163). *Art in the time of the sons of Peisistratos.* Sculpture (165). Relief and architecture (168). *Delphi* (168). Athens (175). *Eretria. Magna Graecia* (175). *Vase-painting. Exekias' late period* (178). *Oltos* (180). *History of the development of amphora shapes* (181). *Influence of the form of government on art* (183). *Attic sculpture in the early years of democracy* (185). *Vase-painting in the early years of democracy* (186). *Persian Wars* (190). *Continuity between Athenian politics and history of Archaic art* (190). *Art, politics and religion* (191). *Religion and philosophy. Nature and art* (193).

APPENDICES . . . . , ... 197–224

Chronological table (198). Captions to Appendix of plates (200). Appendix of plates (201). Notes on the text (209). Glossary (212). Map (214). Index (216).

LIST OF COLOUR PLATES

	Page		Page
Protocorinthian vase	3	Battle with Centaurs	111
Geometric grave amphora	13	Oil vessel	114
Bronze statuette	20	Temple of Apollo, Corinth	123
Late Geometric krater	25	Ionic capital	128
Early Attic krater	27	Funerary statue of Kroisos (Croesus)	131
Cella walls, temple of Hera	32	Fragment of a grave relief	134
Cycladic amphora	39	Centaur	139
Amphora from Eleusis	41	Cauldron handles	142
Bronze plaque from Crete	43	Krater from Vix	144
Protocorinthian perfume flask	46	Hermes carrying a ram	146
Fragment of a relief	51	Bronze statue of Apollo	148
Female figure from Auxerre	54	Amphora by Exekias	153
East Greek animal-frieze jug	57	Clay plate by the painter Lydos	154
Protocorinthian jug, Veii	59	Neck-amphora by Amasis	156
Protocorinthian jug	60	Lekythos by Amasis	159
Bronze statuette, Olympia	64	Chalcidian lidded krater	162
Statuette of a girl from Ephesos	67	Picture on the inside of a cup by Exekias	164
Sepulchral amphora from the Peiraieus	70	Amphora by Exekias	166
Head of the statue of a youth	73	Detail from the frieze of the Siphnian	
Clay metope	78	Treasury	168, 170
Protocorinthian oil-jar	83	Terrace wall, precinct of Apollo at Delphi	174
Lion from a tomb, Corcyra	84	Delphi, sanctuary of Apollo	176
Head of a terracotta sphinx, Calydon	86	Paestum, temple of Athena	179
Figure from a pediment on the Acropolis	92	Calyx krater by Exekias; detail	182
Ornithe, marble statue by Geneleos	96	Fragments of an amphora by Exekias	189
Head of a horseman	102	Amphora by the potter Euxitheos	192
Discus-bearer	104	Picture on the outside of a drinking-cup;	
Calydonian boar hunt	108–9	detail	195

LIST OF FIGURES

	Page		Page
1 – Late Mycenean bull, Attica	15	10 – Artemis; votive offering	56
2 – Terracotta figure of a woman	16	11 – Lyre from Samos	62
3 – Protogeometric stag	17	12 – Temple of Apollo, Thermon	74
4 – Lid of an early Geometric clay pyxis	18	13 – Reconstructed column of the oldest	
5 – Samos, Heraion I	30	temple of Athena Pronaia	75
6 – Statuette of a warrior from the		14 – Reconstruction based on a model of	
Acropolis	44	a temple	77
7 – Types of Greek roof tile	48	15 – Prinias in Crete, ground-plan of	
8/9 – Omphalos cup	49	temple A	77

16 – Porous (limestone) pediment from
    the Acropolis, Athens   88–89
17 – Group of statues by Geneleos   94
18 – Naxian kore   98
19 – Group showing a man leading a cow   99
20 – Sphinx from an Attic tombstone   100
21 – Equestrian statue from Athens   101
22 – Lakonian cup   106
23 – Shield handle from Noicattaro   112
24 – Heraion I   118
25 – Ephesos, Archaic Artemision   120
26 – Altar from Cape Monodendri   122
27 – Corinth, ground-plan of the temple
    of Apollo   122
28 – Metope showing Europa   124
29 – Doric capital of a grave column   125
30 – Aeolic capital   127
31 – Grave stele   127

32 – Inscription from a pillar-capital
    for grave   137
33 – Delphi, ground-plan of the Siphnian
    Treasury   171
34 – Delphi, Siphnian Treasury,
    reconstruction   172
35 – Paestum, temple of Athena   178
36 – Inscribed base of a funerary statue 184
37 – Reliefs on the base of a grave
    monument   187

Figs. 1–4, 6, 8–12, 14–17, 19, 22–24, 26–37 were drawn by Heinz Prüstel, Mainz, and Figs. 18, 20, 21 by F. Barault, Athens, after designs provided by the author. Drawings 5, 7, 13, 25 were taken from the works quoted. The map was prepared by M. Schlatterer, Baden-Baden, after sketches by the author.

ACKNOWLEDGMENTS

The following museums kindly allowed reproduction of the plates on the pages listed below:

Amsterdam, Zoological Museum   39
Argos, Archaeological Museum   25
Athens, Agora Museum   182
Athens, Acropolis Museum   92
Athens, Kerameikos Museum   159
Athens, National Museum   13, 51, 70, 73,
    78, 86, 104, 131, 134, 148, 195
Berlin, Pergamon-Museum   83, 96
Boston, Museum of Fine Arts   57, 146
Boulogne-sur-Mer, Musée d'Archéologie   153
Cambridge (England), Fitzwilliam Museum
                                      67, 142
Châtillon-sur-Seine   144
Delphi   168, 170
Eleusis, Archaeological Museum   41

Florence, Archaeological Museum 108–9, 111
Cercyra   84
London, British Museum   192
Munich, Antikensammlungen 20, 27, 154, 164
New York, Metropolitan Museum   114
New York, Metropolitan Museum, J. Pier-
    pont Morgan Foundation 1917   139
Olympia   64
Paris, Bibliothèque Nationale   156
Paris, Louvre   43, 46, 54, 102
Philadelphia, University Museum   189
Rome, Villa Giulia   3, 59, 60
Samos, Heraion   32, 128
Vatican Museums   166
Würzburg, Martin-v.-Wagner-Museum   162

The colour plates were kindly supplied by: M. Chuzeville, Vanves, p. 43 and 54; H. Devos, Boulogne-sur-Mer, 153; Photo Giraudon, Paris, 102; E. Homann-Wedeking, Munich, 20, 128; J. A. Lavaud, Paris, 13, 123, 179; Foto Scala, Florence, 3, 59, 60, 108–9, 111; Max Seidel, Mittenwald, 25, 41, 51, 64, 70, 73, 84, 86, 104, 131, 134, 148, 154, 162, 164, 168, 170, 174, 176, 182, 195. In the other plates the originals were lent to us for reproduction by the museums concerned.

I. INTELLECTUAL FOUNDATIONS:
THE GEOMETRIC AGE (*circa* 1050–700 B.C.)

To the Greeks of the early historical period all the vessels and utensils made by their predecessors, before the tribes finally settled down, were the household goods of their ancestors. The huge walls of the prehistoric fortresses were explained as the work of the 'Cyclopes'. They stood there, wherever visible remains of them were preserved, as the awe-inspiring legacy of a rationally incomprehensible past, when men had lived 'as they were in those days', days already spoken of by the old man Nestor in the *Iliad* as belonging to a long-forgotten time. The heroes themselves who figured in religious myth and legend projected, with their graves, into the present and received respectful worship. Indeed, on one occasion bones were even found in the grave of one of these mighty men of yore, as Plutarch tells us in connection with the re-burial of Theseus. The age in which the historical memory of the Greeks themselves placed the origin of the name—Hellenes—common to them all, the age in which the Ionic- and Doric-speaking tribes, and then again the Aeolic- and Attic-speaking Ionians, clearly drew apart from each other, signifies, in general terms, the re-founding of the Greek nation. It is manifested in the creation of a new art.

Ceramics Something of the primitive, almost touching look always preserved by prehistoric pots, with their bellying, receptive shape, made without the potter's wheel, is also a characteristic of the technically excellent, sometimes even sophisticated, products of the Cretan potters at the zenith of Minoan civilization. Vessels can be very different. Different shapes and the most various decorations can serve one and the same purpose.

Of course, the wheel was used by most of the potters who worked for the lords of the Mycenean fortresses and Minoan palaces, and also for the population as a whole, in the second millennium before Christ. The evidence for the existence of this technical aid and for its diffusion in Asia Minor and the eastern Mediterranean goes back to the third, perhaps even the fourth, millennium before Christ. But the profile of these clay vessels produced on the potter's wheel seems like a fortuitous section of a continuous curve, part of a wave-like movement dependent on natural laws, not on the human will or an intellectual concept. The decorative ornaments of these vessels are usually of the so-called *en rapport* kind, i.e. patterns which are extensible in all directions; when pictures are painted on the pots the frame and the composition have something indefinite about them—or at any rate the end of the picture does not signify a clear, irrevocable boundary.

PLATE P. 13   We must realize, when we look at an eighth-century B.C. funerary vase, adorned with linear, geometric patterns, a vase which once stood as a memorial on the grave itself, to mark it, that, whereas the materials and technique are the same as those of the Cretan-Mycenean period, the phenomenon of the sepulchral memorial developed out of post-Mycenean prototypes, which were, it is true, much smaller. Nevertheless, something unusually new, something simple and at the same time grandiose, seems suddenly to have appeared, almost without warning. And so in fact it did.

The best way of understanding the phenomenon as a whole is to start by looking at the smallest details. These are the strokes of which the decoration consists. These strokes were made with the greatest precision and confidence. The narrow horizontal lines were probably made by keeping a fine brush fixed against the surface of the vessel as it rotated on the potter's wheel. For the longer horizontal strokes a ruler was certainly employed; the groups of shorter parallel strokes were probably drawn with fine brushes fixed at equal intervals into a handle. Whereas in a somewhat earlier phase of development circles and segments of circles, and above all close concentric circles, form the chief element of decoration, here curved and circular forms occur only rarely. They are replaced, at a most important area in the symmetry of the vase,

Geometric grave amphora from the necropolis outside the double gate of Athens. About 770 B.C. *Height 5 ft. 1 in. Athens, National Museum. Cf. above, pp. 16, 18, 22, 37, 194.*

13

namely in the centre of the handle zone, by figures arranged in a strictly symmetrical pattern.

Themes of the pictures The themes of the pictures on such vases are not chosen at random; they are closely connected with the purpose of the vase, with the deeply religious conception of death and with burial customs whose every detail was a ritual. The chief element is mourning for the dead. But the figures themselves are represented in an abstract, extremely articulated style; in other words, in the same geometric form reflected in every individual ornament and in the ornamentation as a whole.

The significance of the decoration as a whole is most clearly evident in the meander patterns. These continuous, 'retarded', uniform, but never monotonous bands of ornamentation could be compared in their structure with the subtle, yet extraordinarily simply constructed Homeric verse, the dactylic hexameter. Such a comparison provides an important clue to our understanding of the artistic output of this period, precisely because it touches only the most general elements, the fundamental character. It shows that both in painted pictures and in poetry the artistic forms are based on the same presuppositions, namely the imaginative world and the modes of thought of those days. The living human being saw himself not as a single entity but as a harmonious plurality of various physical, psychic, spiritual, active, and above all passive qualities, receptive to impression and experience. The broad meander bands, with their antithetical, angular shape, are as it were a symbol of these manifold powers. Even mutually opposing tendencies are reduced to order in the meander systems. Moreover, the very shape of the vases bearing these ornamental patterns and figures also shares in the formal principle embodied in the meander. This is revealed in the precision of the sharply articulated contour and in the exact correspondence of the individual parts of the vessel to each other, which together form not an organic composition, but one compacted, so to speak, on the crystalline principle.

Ionia and Athens It is not known for certain in which region of Greece the first beginnings of Greek versification are to be sought, but its development into the mature hexameters and distychs of Homer and

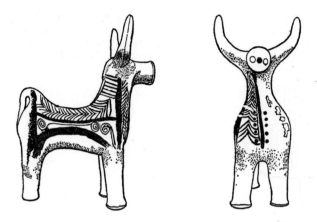

FIG. 1 – *Late Mycenean bull from Attica. Terracotta. Berlin (Prähist. Zeitschrift 19, 1928, 311, Plate 35).*

Archilochos, bound in spite of their simplicity by strict and complex rules, took place in Ionia. The beginnings of 'Geometric' pottery and vase-painting, on the other hand, appear in a city that arose out of the unification of a number of village communities, the city of the Athenians, who prided themselves on being the original inhabitants of their Attic land. However, what is almost more significant about the nature of the new style is that immediately after the first essays it conquered the whole of Greece; the further development and perfection of the forms proceeded simultaneously in almost all Greek territories. Only the more easterly Ionian regions, together with Dorian islands like Rhodes which were enclaves in the Ionian area, never fully embraced Geometric art.

These then are the assumptions we shall make in enquiring into the nature of the people who created and developed the new style. It is natural to ask whether these people left any evidence of themselves in their art. We might expect to find such evidence in sculpture, where the human being is not simply depicted as a silhouette consisting of a number of triangles but modelled in the round.

SMALL-SCALE SCULPTURE

Now it is certainly not due simply to the malevolence of time that large-scale Greek sculpture does not begin to come to our notice until after the first decades of the seventh century B.C.; for in the Geometric period and that immediately preceding it even small-

15

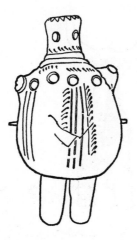

FIG. 2 – *Figure of a woman in terracotta. 10th century B.C. Athens, Kerameikos Museum (Kerameikos, Results of the Excavations, IV, Plate 31, above, centre).*

scale sculpture is relatively scanty. The feeling for large-scale plastic creation found adequate expression in technical and artistic masterpieces like funerary vases as large as a man, which at the same time exemplified perfectly in their shape the specifically Geometric artistic principle. Clay figurines of men and animals come a long way behind. They are still echoes of another, older tradition.

FIG. 1 This is connected with the fact that animal figures in particular were shaped by the same technique as pots. The body was made with the help of the potter's wheel and was furnished with an opening—for example, in the breast—even when the completed object was not going to serve as a plastically modelled vase, as a

FIG. 3 rhyton (drinking vessel) or something of that sort. This hollow cylindrical body was lightly modelled at a number of different places on its surface, then the limbs, neck and head were affixed, and finally the whole was painted and fired. Massive clay figures of

FIG. 2 human beings and animals were more difficult to produce because the bigger volume of clay could not be fired so hard; for there was a much greater danger of the mass cracking and breaking as it contracted during the firing. In any case all these pieces of plastic art are still the products of time-honoured tradition, both in conception and technique; they are not suited to the expression of the new structural principles of Geometric art. It is only when artists begin

16

FIG. 3 – *Protogeometric stag, terracotta. 10th century B.C. Athens, Kerameikos Museum (Kerameikos, Results of the Excavations, IV, Plate 26, above).*

again to think of bronze alloy as a possible material that figures come into being which do belong to Geometric art, yet do not completely follow this inexorably mathematical and clearly conceived formal principle, and above all do not follow this principle alone.

When it comes to parallels with Greek Geometric vase-painting, *Foreign influences* specialized research points to the southern part of the Near East, to the region round Belgrade or even to south central Italy. Nevertheless, it is certain that this new development in Greece was in its own way a native one; it emerged at a creative moment of world significance and was essentially uninfluenced. The bronze statuettes are a different matter. They are unthinkable without Syrian and Old Hittite prototypes, without a 'cultural fallout' from East to West, although, as often happened later too, the original stimulus was absorbed and decisively transformed.

A statuette of a warrior shows an early phase of the new spirit. PLATE P. 20 It is true that what strikes us first about this figure when we look at it without previous preparation is its extreme primitiveness, indeed even perhaps the crudeness with which the means of expression are employed. It is only when one is fairly familiar with the background to figures of this sort dating from those days, when one has some idea of Bronze Age sculpture in Europe and the Near East, and when one also knows that the warrior statuette is virtually

17

FIG. 4 – *Lid of an early Geo-metric clay pyxis with a handle in the shape of a horse. Athens, Kerameikos Museum (F. Matz, Frühgriech. Kunst, I, Plate 26).*

contemporaneous with the monumental vases and also with the earliest Greek temples, that one begins to understand what is so special about this bronze figure, and this means neither more nor less than its significance in world history. The question of *whom* the figure represents must come second to the simpler one of what it represents. In describing it, we must naturally employ *our* vision, *our* modes of thought, *our* paraphrases, but we must not think for a moment that the statuette could have been seen with the same eyes or described with the same words in the early part of the first millennium before Christ.

Before us stands erect a slender man, apparently naked except for a double 'belt' and a helmet, which itself is not very clear, though its serrated crest is. The man stands quietly, with legs slightly apart; the upper arms are stretched out horizontally from the body, and the forearms and hands are raised. On the flattish face the eyes and mouth are each indicated by a horizontal groove, and each knee is similarly shown by two grooves. The fingers, five on each hand, and the toes (four on each foot) are represented by little points corresponding in shape to the points or teeth of the crest on the helmet. By means of the pegs still preserved under the feet the statuette was either fixed to a base of its own or else attached to a utensil or piece of furniture.

Quite apart from the differences in *genre* and size, the warrior also PLATE P. 13 shows, in comparison with the funerary vase, a clear difference in quality. From a purely technical point of view, as a piece of ceramic, the vase is an almost incredible masterpiece. And in the composition of the decoration—the picture of the lying in state and lamentation of the dead, and the two animal friezes—the painter is fully the equal of the potter. The vessel was made in the leading pottery centre of the time, in Athens, and the best trained and most lucid artists of the period finished it off. The bronze statuette, on the other hand, certainly has a decidedly provincial air about it. Yet the common Greek element and the attitude of the age find equally clear expression in both works.

Geometric ornamentation, especially the meander, is so characteristic of the pottery that the whole period from about 1050 to 700 B.C. has been christened 'the Geometric period'. However, geometry as the art of measuring, as a science and mode of thought, is two-dimensional (even spherical geometry is based primarily on the plane surface), while sculpture occupies space and extends into three dimensions. What is represented in two-dimensional art by simple Geometric forms is correspondingly expressed in sculpture by *stereometric* forms. The beginnings of this mode of artistic construction, displayed in perfection by somewhat later bronze statuettes, can be detected in the statuette of the warrior. The body has scarcely any volume. It is not, so to speak, the figure as such which is represented, but rather its constructional framework, a sort of skeleton, though one, it is true, that is thoroughly oriented in space. The main part of this orientation is played by a certain symmetry and a preference for the right angle, both in the vertical and in the horizontal plane. The stylization of the human figure in Greek Geometric—and also, for example, Egyptian—two-dimensional art has been very aptly described as the 'alternate view': while the head and legs appear in profile, the breast is shown frontally. This is a convention that only has—and can have—any point in two-dimensional art. In contrast to this, even a provincial statuette, in which the substance, as a modelled mass, makes hardly any appearance at all, is *plastic*, that is, spatial. Now it cannot be asserted that a continuous line of development can be traced from the germ of stereometric form evident in the statuette down to a statue carved PLATE P. 131

19

Bronze statuette of a warrior. *9th century* B.C. *Height* 5⁴/5 *in. Munich,*
Antikensammlungen. Cf. pp. 17 ff., 28.

300 years later, but we can use, in the interpretation of the statuette, a number of definitions which throw a good deal of light on the real essence of figures much later in date.

The artist works with formulas, which may also be called—to make our meaning more precise—ideograms. Grooves incised with the chisel indicate eyes, mouth and knees; the crest denotes the helmet, and the 'belt' probably the lower edge of the armour, the rest of which is not shown; the jagged teeth indicate fingers, toes and the bristling crest of the helmet. The raised arms, the open hands are a religious gesture signifying prayer, and also the appearance of the divinity invoked by the prayer—the epiphany. But what gives the figure unity of form and thus makes it into a work of art is its living dynamic. This is displayed in the slight deviations from strict symmetry, in the mobile flow of the stereometric forms (in spite of the statuette's tranquil attitude), in the unified symbolic character of the formulas already mentioned, and above all in the expressive force of these formulas. It is obvious at first glance that the intention is not just to portray *any* human figure, but a man, still more precisely a warrior, and finally—as the position of the arms makes clear—a warrior in the realm of religion, that is, a worshipper or a god.

It is natural to ask what kind of human community, what religious and sociological assumptions, produced a figure like this.

Religious and sociological background

Apart from the numerous indications for which we are indebted to archaeological investigation of the various cultural strata in the soil, the most important source for the answer to this question is the *Iliad*. People's lives were determined by the mighty warrior; he represented and protected the community. Although the great female divinities in particular show traces of a native or oriental mother-worship—or even a vegetation cult—the Olympian gods are primarily personal beings raised to the highest degree of perfection. Zeus, lord of the world and god of lightning, is a warrior —he wore a helmet (Pausanias v, 17, 1)—and so is his son Apollo, the purest symbol of new, *Greek* religious feeling. The warrior's calling necessitated special craftsmen, smiths, who probably specialized in particular weapons. Doctors were the next need, as surgeons in case of emergency. Of course, smiths also made agricultural and household tools. There were also wood-carvers and carpenters, musicians and singers; the existence of painters and potters has already been implied. Thus there was a varied class of craftsmen and, if you like, artists. But the economic foundation of life was still agriculture; the great mass of the people were farmers. In addition to agriculture, there was also fishing and hunting.

The princes who protected those who dwelt around them by means of their physical strength, their courage and their skill in the use of arms were the real owners of all sources of wealth, especially landed property. It was a patriarchal monarchy, which at several focal points in different localities probably became an urban monarchy during the course of the ninth century. The Athenians, who had the most strongly developed sense of history of all the Greeks, saw this event in terms of the unification of several separate villages in one proper urban settlement, an achievement which they ascribed to King Theseus.

Of course, circumstances varied in detail from one region to another and the rhythm of historical development was not the same everywhere, but on the whole the mode of life and the kind of community we have outlined prevailed all over Greece in the Geometric age. PLATE P. 13 How much of this life was reflected in art? In the vase-paintings with their numerous figures we have already recognized burial scenes; in other words, not mythological pictures, but stylized, refined reproductions of contemporary life. To the same category belong the chariots and drivers which encircle so many vases with scarcely any variation of type; they represent funeral and mourning processions rather than races arranged near the grave or funeral pyre. The land and sea battles may be regarded as the preliminaries to all these sepulchral events; if they are often perhaps more symbolic than realistic in character, providing a kind of general reminder of the inevitability of death, the same is true of the pictures of hunting expeditions that ended in disaster and of tragic shipwrecks. Pictures of sport and music can be understood as representations of competitions, which were also part of the cult of the dead. Whereas all these pictures occur on vases which were either placed on top of the grave or put inside the grave with the deceased, most of the contemporary clay and bronze statuettes come from sanctuaries. But are they votive figures depicting the donors or likenesses of the gods? In most cases it is impossible to decide for certain, though it would probably be right to regard the little bronze groups from Olympia, which portray a team and charioteer, sometimes with a heavily armed companion, not as gods but as portraits of human benefactors which were dedicated at the sanctuary. But it is only towards the end of the Geometric period that the significance of these works becomes quite unequivocal: a smith beating out a helmet on a little anvil can scarcely represent Hephaistos! A little later it is quite clear from the inscription and from the dress of a bronze statuette which can be dated to about 700 B.C. that it represents Apollo.

However, in the Geometric period bronze statuettes of animals precede and outnumber by far those of human beings. Commonest are little horses and small votive statues of cattle. It is among the *FIG. 4* animal figures, too, that one can most easily distinguish separate stylistic groups and ascribe them to different regions. The main workshops seem to have been Argos, Corinth and Sparta; thus this *Argos, Corinth* development seems to have taken place mainly in the Peloponnesian *and Sparta* peninsula. Thessaly and the Cyclades were also concerned in it, but are less fruitful. There is a parallel here with the regional distribution of the potteries and their respective significance for Greece as a whole. One important difference must be noted, however: whereas in Geometric vase-painting Athens is the uncontested leader, in the technique and artistic application of bronze-casting it lags some distance behind the other workshops.

Once Athens had come into existence it became the political and *Attica* cultural centre of Attica. Whoever wished to rule Attica had first to make himself lord of Athens. It was also the source of all the intellectual and artistic impulses, impulses whose influence was often felt beyond the frontiers of Attica. However, we must realize that the influential families were not really by origin and domicile urban ones, but landed nobility with large estates. The theoretical implication of this seems to be that certain aristocratic houses in

Attica may have been centres of social and political life, and even centres of artistic activity. This deduction has been confirmed by finds made in the relatively remote but fertile country districts. The quality of the works of art, even of the earliest period, discovered in such areas is fully equal, if not in some cases superior, to that of the best finds from the city of Athens itself.

Thus the contents of graves found in the neighbourhood of Eleusis are amazing in their technical and artistic perfection. They consist of vessels of the early, so-called Protogeometric phase and also examples of the somewhat later Black Dipylon ware. Of course, Eleusis occupies in any case a special position among the Attic communities because of the importance of its very ancient cult of Demeter. But no such religious reasons exist to distinguish, for example, the district of Anavyssos from other similar villages. Here for centuries some of the best Archaic statues have been found and the cemetery is rich in ceramic masterpieces of the years after 600 B.C. But that is not all: in recent years rich and unexpected finds of first-quality Geometric ware have also been made in its graves. The contents of these graves are distinguished not just by wealth and mere luxury, but primarily by the finest artistic taste in both conception and execution; those who commissioned these works were people with clear ideas and a high level of intelligence. It is true that no differences in style can be detected in the works of art found at the various sites in Attica; the style is everywhere the common Attic one. Differences, sometimes clearly perceptible, only come to light when we compare finds from different regions, which show characteristic variations according to their geographical location and also according to the race and language of their populations.

Artistic regions These spheres of artistic activity, whose boundaries are clearly defined even in the Geometric age, are, in addition to the Attic region, the Boeotian, the Thessalian, the Corinthian, the Argive, the Cycladic, the Cretan and the East Greek. The artistic individuality of Attica has already revealed itself, in several examples, as consisting in precise contours, firm structure and clear drawing; we shall therefore confine ourselves here simply to showing an

24

Late Geometric krater from Argos. Second half of 8th century B.C. *Diameter 1 ft. 8 in. Argos, Archaeological Museum. Cf. below.*

example of the different nature of Geometric art in Argos, namely, PLATE ABOVE a squat, very broad vase with so-called 'bow-shaped' handles. In form and decoration it shows close ties with the Attic amphora; the shape of the Argive vase can be regarded as that of a vertically compressed, widely bulging amphora. The later date of the painting is revealed by the reservation of the horses' eyes and the men's

25

faces—as opposed to the full silhouette of the early Geometric period—and also by the introduction of the zigzag bands and the spiral motif. Typically Argive is the central motif between the framed figures, namely the stepped meander; the right-angled hooks which run down vertically by the men leading the horses are to be explained typologically as extracts from this kind of meander. But what is particularly characteristic of Argos is the curious restlessness of the drawing as a whole. The relationship of the separate parts of the decoration to each other lacks the iron firmness displayed by the Attic vase. The composition both as a whole and in detail is neither so immovably firm nor so clear as at Athens. This is not because the Argive vase is later; it is indeed later, as we have seen, but the reason for the differences with which we are now concerned lies not in chronology but in geography.

PLATE P. 27 Even a considerably later Attic vase-painting—just look at the stylization of the horse's mane!—has the clarity and firmness of the older pictorial and ornamental composition which are missing in the Argive vessel. On the other hand, on the Argive krater all the decorative elements are crowded more closely together. It is true that in Attica too, at a certain stage of development in the eighth century, the vases with both figures and ornamental motifs are more richly covered than in the early period of Geometric art. Nevertheless, they still reflect the criteria we have mentioned—clarity, precision and firmness. Moreover, something that always distinguishes Attic Geometric vases from those of other regions is the position of the figure picture—when there is one at all—on the surface of the vase. In Attica the figures are always placed centrally, in the most important zone of the decoration, and in the middle of this zone; and from here they show a clear tendency to determine the rest of the decoration. In the products of other potteries the figures tend to be only accessory. For example, on the Argive krater there are two figure pictures, but they frame a purely ornamental motif that is the real centre of the composition. The pictures show men leading horses. This motif, and pictures of horses in general, occur very frequently on Argive vases. 'Horse-rearing Argos', Homer calls it. It can certainly be assumed that these pictures,

Early Attic krater (detail). First quarter of 7th century B.C. *Height of vase 15³/5 in. Munich, Antiken-sammlungen. Cf. pp. 26, 37, 38.*

too, have some sepulchral significance, although they are not very clearly characterized in this respect. The artistic products of the various different regions do not differ in significance or function, but in style. The Argive style is not distinguished from the Attic simply by the absence of Attic marks of quality. The wealth of decorative elements, the variation and development of decorative forms—to the point of fragmentation and even dissolution, the emphatic equality of ornament and figure, and the vitality which every single motif seems, as it were, to radiate, all give the Argive vase the stamp of high ceramic quality. At the same time these features reflect an artistic independence which is also found in the eastern and northern parts of the Greek world, and above all at Sparta and Corinth. During the *Geometric* age, it is true, all these regions are extensively influenced by Attica, but when Geometric art moves into its final phase, and in Attica itself the figure picture and the portrayal of human beings—which in the long run does not really fit in with strict geometric stylization—lead to the break-up of the Geometric style, the situation changes. The previously suppressed peculiarities of other peoples and cities emerge into the limelight with an already developed programme and aims already implicit earlier.

ARMOUR   The craft of the armourer has already been mentioned. Argos, as it happens, has left us evidence of its achievements in this field during the Geometric age, in the shape of a piece of work that could APPX. PL. 8   well be contemporary with the Argive krater. We shall also see later how in the sixth century the equipment of the warriors in vase-paintings corresponds so completely with the arms actually preserved that we are quite justified in making deductions from the pictures about the weapons really used in those days, even in cases where parts of the equipment are not known, or not sufficiently known, from archaeological discoveries. The situation is quite different in the Geometric period. Between the statuette of the PLATE P. 20   Thessalian warrior on the one hand and the helmet and breastplate from the Argive grave on the other there is a great gap which makes the degree of stylization present in artistic forms quite evident. Men's clothing and also their armour naturally served practical ends in the first place. But over and above this the warrior in the finery of his helmet and the radiance of shield, sword and spear becomes himself almost a work of art stylized by the armourer. This creation, this living statue, so to speak, can only be accommodated very imperfectly to the formal conventions of the Geometric style. The warrior of the late Archaic period, the Roman legionary, the Renaissance knight all lend themselves much more easily to the feeling for form in their respective periods. The heavily armed soldier of the Greek early period, on the other hand, in all the weight and splendour of his weapons, differs to our eyes very

28

substantially from contemporary representations of him. But perhaps it is only to our eyes that he differs, for it must be repeated once again that we simply do not know *a priori* how the Greeks of the ninth and eighth centuries saw themselves and their warriors; we can only try to deduce this from the artistic works that have been preserved.

One might think that in architecture the mathematical and constructive elements in Geometric vases and pictures would re-appear, and this is to a certain extent the case. However, what is true of sculpture is also true of architecture: in the centuries after 1000 B.C. it is primarily received traditions that continue to run their course. The 'megaron' type of house, already known to us from the oldest strata of Troy and later from the Mycenean age in the Peloponnese, lived on; we still meet it in a slightly altered form in the seventh and sixth centuries, and indeed even in the fifth. Moreover, there is an undeniable resemblance, at a certain stage in its development, between the simple Doric *templum in antis* and the megaron. But when the Greek temple containing a base for a statue, and therefore obviously a dwelling for the god, first appears—in Ionia, according to the evidence at our disposal—it is a new creation that owes nothing to any tradition.

It is possible that the earliest examples of such temples were made of wood and have therefore disappeared completely. If so, they were probably extremely small and modest in format in comparison with the oldest of those whose remains have been preserved or whose designs can be deduced. The creation of Greek architecture proper, the greatest achievement of which was in fact the temple, became a pressing necessity at the moment when the gods were no longer omnipresent, when they had withdrawn from the ever-existing possibility of direct manifestation into an image full of magical power, which soon ceases to be the god himself and simply denotes him. It is the statue of the god that creates the need for the temple. A powerful female divinity belonging to the oriental religions was turned by the Greeks into Hera, the bride of heaven. It can hardly be a coincidence that the earliest Greek temples known to us are dedicated to her. One lies in the heart of Ionia, on the island of

ARCHITECTURE

Cult of Hera and temples of Hera

Samos, which was already rich in the Bronze Age; another in Dorian Olympia, the centre of the Hellenic national festivals. A third adopts the architectural tradition of the second millennium from the citadel of Tiryns. Its original cult image of pear wood, a statue of Hera in a sitting position, was transferred to the most famous of all Heraia, the Heraion of Argos, the place regarded by the Greeks as the home of the whole cult of Hera. These temples show no signs at all of the later canonical forms, yet they differ from all older sacred or profane buildings of the Mediterranean area.

FIG. 5 The old temple of Hera on Samos was rebuilt several times. Only the first version, which can be dated to the eighth century—probably somewhere around 750 B.C.—will be described here. It was a strikingly long building, with a ground-plan which forms a rectangle about 39 yards long and nearly 8 yards wide. The remains comprise parts of the wall foundations, consisting of flat slabs of limestone, the foundations of some of the pillars which divided the interior into two aisles—there were no exterior columns or pillars in the first version of the building—and the base of a cult statue, which stands somewhat eccentrically at the end of the long corridor-like space in such a position that only part of the statue of the goddess was hidden by the line of interior pillars from anyone entering.

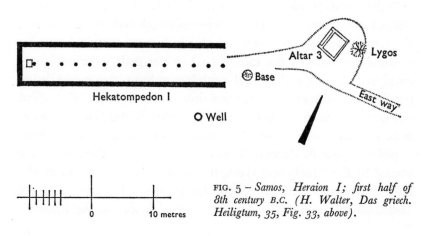

FIG. 5 – *Samos, Heraion I; first half of 8th century B.C. (H. Walter, Das griech. Heiligtum, 35, Fig. 33, above).*

30

These interior supports are certainly explained by the need for their assistance in spanning the width of the cella, which was narrow, it is true, but posed considerable structural problems. On the other hand, it is uncertain whether the line of 14 wooden posts, which should be imagined as beams with a rectangular section rather than as columns, form a strong enough argument for assuming that the roof was a ridged one. A flat roof, possibly with a layer of earth on it, is also a possibility. In any case, roof tiles were not yet known at that time. Thus if the roof was ridged, it must have been a relatively steep one of woven brushwood and layers of reeds. If this remains an open question, it must also be admitted that we can only guess at the material and technique used for the walls of the building. It is probable that a good deal of wood was used in the building as a whole, as has already been implied in our attempt to describe what it must have looked like. According to the legend, even the statue of the goddess herself was a miraculously discovered piece of wood. On the basis of this inconclusive evidence, are we in a position to assert the special importance of this temple in the history of architecture?

The most peculiar thing about it is the elongated ground-plan; the proportion of breadth to length is 1:5. This means that those entering found themselves at a relatively great distance from the cult statue, which stood in the dim light at the far end of a long corridor, partly hidden by the line of supporting pillars. But perhaps the rectangular tunnel (for that is more or less what the interior must have looked like), with its division into two narrow aisles, also exerted a sort of magic emotional spell that sucked the worshipper in, as it were, when he crossed the threshold.

It is the other way about if one imagines oneself standing by the side of the small, roughly hewn stones which formed the substructure for the base of the cult statue—the upper block on which the wooden image actually rested has not been preserved. Here, in the depths of the long, dark, eastward-facing space, stood the wooden Hera, dressed every year in fresh robes, 'enveloped' in the twigs of the tree sacred to her, hung with necklaces, and possibly also garlanded with vine leaves. Framed by the bright opening of the

South-west corner of the cella walls of the second temple of Hera. First half of 7th century B.C. *Samos, Heraion. Cf. p. 33.*

forty-yard distant entrance was the living symbol of the goddess, the lygos, the sacred tree of Hera. This tree grew immediately behind the altar, which faced north-west and was visible in our imagined field of vision, though only diagonally, thus enabling the goddess to take part 'visibly' in the sacrificial rites.

If one tries in this way to visualize the facts and the conclusions they suggest, it becomes clear that the old temple of Hera on Samos has a special significance not only in the history of architecture but also in the history of religion. The Greek temple comes into being when part of the divine power is compressed into an image, at first one not even formed by human hands; for an image needs a temple. And this temple takes a very simple, functional form, but a highly compressed and expressive one. The plastic Greek architectural unit has been created. Here, at its first appearance, it almost gives the impression of being an enlarged prototype of a marble block of the Periclean age, the basic unit of which the later 'classical' buildings were composed.

Parts of this oldest of Greek temples have been preserved, as if by a miracle—not only parts of the foundations, but also one of the stones from the walls and above all the masonry substructure for the base of the temple statue. All this is covered over, it is true, by stones of the succeeding building, erected at the beginning of the seventh century, but as this retained the size and proportions of the older temple it provides important data for reconstructing it. The later building, which certainly had a ridged roof, also dispensed, in its final version, with interior supports; there is evidence that the last phase of the older building already had a line of exterior supports, or peristyle.

What is visible today at first sight makes a very modest impression. PLATE P. 32 It is the south-west corner, that is, the southern part of the rear wall of the temple house, the cella. One must attempt a reconstruction, either on paper or in the imagination, in order to understand how well the narrow, finely tooled blocks are one and all worthy of the spirit and proportions of the nicely calculated whole, how the carefully laid top course of the foundations, and the wall, four courses of which have been preserved at one place, reflect an architecture of mature craftsmanship which is amazing in the subtlety of its harmonies. Originally there were even wall-paintings, too; a block with a design for a painted frieze scratched on it has been preserved. The subject of the painting was a festal procession of men carrying spears; obviously the cult procession from the city of Samos to the sanctuary nearly five miles away, a procession in which the citizens carried arms. As only the top strip of the frieze has been preserved, showing the heads of the figures and the tops of the spears at fairly wide intervals, it may have been a frieze of horsemen. If this frieze was affixed to the wall at the height at which friezes usually appear in temples of the Ionic order, then this block is proof that in this second temple of Hera the cella walls were built completely of stone. In any case, this second temple does not belong in any way to the Geometric period; rather is it one of the testimonies to the transformation, the renewal of modes of life and artistic styles by which, after the end of the Geometric period, a new age was slowly but steadily brought into being.

II. REVOLUTION AND CONSOLIDATION:
THE ORIENTALIZING AGE
(*circa* 700–620 B.C.)

A Geometric sense of order always remained the innermost core of Greek art right to the end, but the externally Geometric forms began to break up towards the end of the eighth century. And the firmer, the more inviolable these forms had been, the more violent was the shock. Naturally the collapse of Geometric art was not the occasion or the reason for the shock, but *vice versa*, the consequence or a symptom of the shock. The shock itself probably first became apparent in the political structure, and may even have originated there. In most of the Greek states power shifted from the hereditary monarchy to the nobles. All over Greece, with the exception of Sparta, kings were replaced by a system of aristocratic rule, which differed in its precise form from place to place. Naturally the change could not take the form of a smooth transition. Almost everywhere it was accompanied by struggles for power—sometimes even a revolution; by struggles for power which dragged on in some places for decades among the noble families, or else flared up again at varying intervals. Often, after a long tug-of-war between the different parties, this struggle ended in the form of government known as 'tyranny'.

At the same time this age of political change is also marked by both active and passive expansion. The age of Geometric forms had been a world closed in on itself; but as these tranquil, interlocking, firmly fixed forms change into the new, no longer Geometric but already basically organic ones—in other words, into forms that are, in the narrower sense of the term, Archaic—there is clear evidence of stronger influence from the Near East. Into the world of the Greeks, whose political structure was in many places undergoing fundamental change at this time, who were sending out bold colonists eastward and westward from the poor soil of the homeland, and who were assimilating oriental ideas in their cosmic and philosophical conceptions, came merchants and artists from the

Break-up of Geometric art forms

Political background

Foreign influences

35

East. Above all the Greeks themselves, urged on by the desire to widen their physical and intellectual horizons, travelled to the East. Greek artists came to know other techniques and other materials, ivory in particular, and also, of course, a world of imagery totally different from that with which they were familiar. Much of all this they took over. But nothing was taken over that was not capable of being fundamentally transformed. From this fusion of native and foreign elements the Archaic style of the Greeks was born. In spite of all the external stimuli and all the foreign models, the creation of this style was without question a purely Greek achievement.

Crete There was—and still is—a widespread view that the southern Greek island of Crete played a leading part in this renewal of artistic style. In the last few decades attempts have been made, with some success, to ascribe a leading rôle in the process to the islands which lie in that part of the eastern Mediterranean known as the Aegean Sea. These are the numerous, often rocky islands *Cyclades* called the Cyclades, whose religious centre was Delos. On Delos, according to the hymn, the goddess Leto gave birth to the twins Apollo and Artemis. Thenceforth Delos was always the sacred island of Apollo. At any rate, the Cyclades were certainly one of the Greek regions which, in the political and artistic innovations of this period, put their own stamp on the products of Greek art. *Corinth, East Greece* Other such regions were the Peloponnese, especially Corinth; the *and Athens* East Greek areas of Asia Minor and the islands just off the coast of Asia Minor; and finally Attica and Athens, even though they now lost their monopoly. In this period, also known, because of the above-mentioned contacts with the East, as the orientalizing age, these four regions were centres of development. The *one* centre of the early period, Athens, is now replaced by four, each of which makes very different use of the borrowed eastern forms. Yet fundamentally all four regional styles, different and characteristically individual though they are, remain genuinely Greek. The strongest proof of this is the fact that they display only the intellectual content which we know already from Geometric art, treated in various ways and put together so as to form a different aggregate, so to speak. By far the biggest body of evidence for this development, which we can follow almost without a break in all the four orientalizing artistic centres of Greece, is provided by vase-painting. Let us look, for example, at the grazing stag on a vase-painting of the first half of the seventh century B.C. The long-legged animal with its tense outlines is scarcely at all reminiscent of the Geometric 'silhouette style'. The old pictorial scheme, employed earlier for purely ornamental purposes, has been transferred to the field of organic life. Yet the ancestry of this realistically modelled, if strictly stylized, animal is perfectly clear. The line of descent runs from the striding ibexes of the big Attic grave amphora via pictures of stags on the edges of Geometric cups down to the long-legged horses of late Geometric figure pictures, which already border on so-called proto-Attic painting. In both the Geometric and the later pictures the relationship between the natural model and the stylized reproduction is similar. The artist does not try to give us a direct impression of a picture seen and grasped in a moment, as did the painters—especially the fresco painters—of the Minoan palaces in Crete in the second millennium B.C. The Greek artist forms a sort of inner idea of the animal, to be depicted by means of innumerable, very precise, isolated observations, and it is this idea, composed only of essential and characteristic individual features, that is reproduced in the picture. In Geometric art this process becomes quite simply one of abstraction, but even in Greek art of the seventh century B.C. a good deal of abstraction persists, for here, too, we are given not a direct optical impression but a type put together by an intellectual process out of numerous individual specimens. The life possessed by these pictures is thus not natural, directly depicted life, but rather the vitality of an intellectual act of creation, which is needed in order to bring the picture of the *type* into existence. The process of development and thus the gradual alteration of the type is of course influenced not only by new and different observations of the natural model but also by every artistic representation of this same type that has once been created and become known. The situation is similar, or at any rate not different in principle, when the point of departure is not a model from nature but an

CERAMICS

APPX. PL. I

PLATE P. 13

PLATE P. 27

37

already existing work of art—an oriental prototype, for example. The amphora with the picture of the stag was made on one of the islands of the Cyclades group. So far it has not been possible to define its place of origin more precisely. On the other hand, it is certain that other vases belong to the same stylistic group and PLATE P. 39 probably come from the same workshop. Two of these vases show in one case a crouching and in the other a squatting lion. The outline of all these vases is simpler than that of Geometric pots; at the same time it no longer gives the impression of being formed once and for all, as though with a metal template, but displays the counterplay of different tensional components. In clarity of contour, however, these vases are fully the equal of Geometric pots. But the way in which the figure picture, too, differs from its Geometric predecessors can be defined in the same words as those applied to the execution of the outline. A comparison will show how in the Cyclades the formal uncertainty, indeed even confusion of style, which followed the end of the Geometric age, was quickly overcome and transformed into new and noble forms. The interval PLATE P. 27 of time between the teams of the Munich krater and the stag in Stockholm is certainly not very great; yet whereas the Attic horses can only be adduced as evidence of a late style, of the final phase of Geometric painting, the stag testifies to new ability—the ability first to observe animal life and organic movement, and secondly to reproduce this observation, by means of the above-mentioned intellectual act of creation, in the simple, unified, vital, but also in their own way abstract forms of the Archaic style. Very many of the later Archaic pictures of animals belong, not only in content but also in form, to the line of development of which the Cycladic stag is one of the earliest specimens: for example, the horse on the APPX. PL. 15 Lakonian cup in London, or the horses on the bronze krater in PLATE P. 144 Châtillon-sur-Seine, or those—in much more violent movement, it is true—on the clay krater in Würzburg.

PLATE P. 162 The period during which artists in the Cyclades were already able to work successfully with such noble yet at the same time such simple forms—about 680–670 B.C.—is at Athens marked to a large extent by artistic experiments rather than by completely valid

Cycladic amphora. First half of 7th century B.C. *Height 21 in. Amsterdam, Zoological Museum. Cf. p. 38.*

PLATE P. 41

achievements. But these Athenian products include such very bold efforts as the dramatic picture of the blinding of Polyphemos. The scene is based on Homer's description of the incident (*Odyssey*, IX, 370–400). Odysseus, assisted by two comrades, is thrusting the glowing point of the huge stake into the eye of the drunken giant. The figure of the wily hero is picked out in white paint. The uncouth monster Polyphemos, sitting down and leaning back, is characterized by streaky use of dark colour. The whole incident is very strikingly depicted, especially the organic mobility of the Greek wanderer's limbs, with their contours swelling somewhat meaninglessly. The style of the picture may be described as expressionist, and the ambitious painter was certainly aiming much higher than the painters of the somewhat older stag and lion pictures. But these extravagantly expressive pictures by Attic painters of this period came to grief on the problem of proportions and artistic economy, and sometimes even on the problem of harmony between the shape of the vase and its decoration.

At any rate, in the seventh century B.C. Attica was less directly affected by foreign influences than other Greek regions. For example, even *Crete* shows evidence of much greater importations from the East on a much larger scale. There native production, too, is much more varied. Besides survivals of old Minoan forms of the second millennium, in the so-called Eteo-Cretan style, there are imitations of oriental prototypes as well as regional variations of genuinely Greek, Dorian art and above all a very individual early Archaic, specifically Cretan style, most beautifully exemplified by fine bronze

PLATE P. 43

engravings and some carved bronze plaques, found only in Crete and depicting not mythical scenes but scenes from life, from everyday life, if you like. Here one gains an insight into a mature development. The perfection of the proportions and contours of the individual figures and the beautifully balanced composition of the two-figure groups are unequalled in the whole of Greek art. These artists, who worked without exception on a fairly small scale, were fully conscious both of the scope and of the limits of their means. The slenderness of the figures, their springy step, the facing pose, the elegant way in which they behave towards each other, all go

Odysseus blinds Polyphemos. Picture on the neck of an amphora from Eleusis. Second quarter of 7th century B.C. *Height of vase 4 ft. 8 in. Eleusis, Archaeological Museum. Cf. p. 40.*

to make these bronze plaques into cabinet pieces of a craft with very ancient traditions and of the most refined taste. Admittedly, the Cretans never created a monumental form in the proper sense of the term; it is possible that they never even tried to do so. This is also true to a certain extent of the Dorian areas of the Peloponnese. Although Corinth was the most productive artistic centre in Greece during the seventh century, although in ceramics the Corinthian potters and vase-painters broke the Attic monopoly from the end of the Geometric period onwards and throughout the century retained a pre-eminent position in vase decoration—and, significantly, also in the export of vases—the masterpieces of the highest quality tend to be the smaller pots. In view of the thousands of examples that have been preserved, this cannot be regarded as a coincidence; the artists concerned must have consciously and expressly practised this limitation in outward size.

It is not difficult to enumerate a very large number of such characteristic masterpieces. Particularly important for the history of art are those in which one can compare, in the same piece, the development of two-dimensional art—vase-painting—with the development of three-dimensional creations—small-scale sculpture. For clay and bronze statuettes, too, the end of the Geometric age meant at first only the loss of a clear syntax of forms. Much tentative experimentation was needed, and a certain period of time had to elapse, before the new, Archaic style was created in this branch of art. It can be asserted today that from the moment that Greece came to know life-size sculpture its artistic development was governed by large-scale sculpture. There are statuettes whose stylistic character reveals clearly that when they were made there were as yet no really big statues in existence; in the same way, we possess pieces of miniature sculpture which by their very pose imply the existence of contemporary or earlier large-scale prototypes. Among the latter is the spout of an almost miniature perfume flask in the shape of a woman's head; an example of the former is an Attic

Relationship between small-scale and large-scale sculpture

PLATE P. 46

Bronze plaque from Crete. Second quarter of 7th century B.C. *Height 7 in. Paris, Louvre. Cf. p. 40.*

FIG. 6 bronze statuette made in the interval, as it were, between Geometric and orientalizing art, about 700 B.C.

The bronze statuette—again of a warrior—is full of a much stronger vitality than the Geometric bronze of a warrior discussed earlier. This vitality reaches out into space, as is shown by the 'spread-out style' in which the figure is composed: the legs are parted and the outstretched arms are bent in different directions; originally the right arm held a spear and the left a shield. But that is not all: there is something aggressive about the statuette's whole attitude, and the starting point of this dynamic composition is the challenging, thrusting look of the wide-set eyes, which are modelled in relief. The wild, indeed undisciplined, look of this statuette points forward to Attic vase-paintings like the picture of Odysseus described above. In complete contrast to this kind of modelling is the head that PLATE P. 46 crowns the little perfume flask. It has rightly been said that this little statue, only an inch or two high, embodies the concept of 'inner monumentality'. The proportions have gained firmness, the plastic surface is an inviolable boundary between inner movement and the neutral space all round it. Whence did such creations draw their form and their lasting content? With the appearance of large-scale sculpture, Greek art was transformed. This change was absorbed by the various individual regions of Greece sometimes sooner and sometimes later, and by individual artists sometimes consciously and sometimes unconsciously. But once the new dimension becomes visible every piece of sculpture, whether big or small, has a share in it.

No other Greek city has left us so many seventh-century vases as Corinth, and no other city exported so many vases, mainly to the Greek colonies in southern Italy and Sicily. And since the foundation dates of these colonies enable us to establish a chronological framework, the various phases of Corinthian vase-painting can be dated within relatively narrow limits. From the pictures on it, the little perfume flask in Paris can be placed in the years round 650 B.C.

FIG. 6 – *Statuette of a warrior from the Acropolis. Bronze. Early 7th century B.C. Athens, National Museum (Ath. Mitt., 1930, supplement XLIV, left).*

Protocorinthian perfume flask from Thebes. Middle of 7th century B.C.
Height 2⁷/₁₀ in. Paris, Louvre. Cf. pp. 42, 44, 49, 115.

In spite of its tiny height the vase bears two friezes of figures. The lower one shows a pack of hounds gaily chasing a hare; the upper one contains a picture from legend—the struggle for a fallen warrior and other heroic duels. It is on Corinthian vases that numerous themes from the legends concerning gods and heroes appear for the first time. This in itself testifies to the imagination and artistic ability of the Corinthians. In this connection it should also be emphasized that it is on Corinthian vases that the figure of Athena armed with a spear first appears—the picture of the Attic Athena Promachos—long before it was known in Athens. This armed Athena, who was also the patroness of Sparta, is obviously the immediate successor of a 'shield goddess' of the second millennium, whose picture has come down to us on a seal ring and on a painting on stucco from Mycenae.

In early Greek culture innovations, technical and artistic 'discoveries', by which every now and then a new tradition is founded, are a sure sign of intellectual concentration, of artistic activity. *Technical innovations* Thus in the field of vase-painting it is particularly important that, according to the archaeological evidence, the black-figure technique was first employed in Corinth. This term means that most of the figures and objects in the pictures appear as completely black areas in which the interior details are inserted by scratching (probably with a hard metal stylus) after the firing, in such a way that the clay background is exposed again. The limitless possibilities inherent in the use of this technique were soon recognized and the technique itself quickly spread to other workshops, including, about 630, the potteries of Athens. But this is only one of the 'discoveries' that can be placed to the credit of the Corinthians. According to later tradition, sculpture in clay had been practised intensively at Corinth and it was also there that the beginnings of relief sculpture were to be sought. The decoration of antefixes with faces in relief is regarded as a Corinthian discovery; and a system of flat tiles with angular covering tiles, every one of which is ridged, is known as a Corinthian roof. A further discovery was of the highest importance FIG. 7 to Greek art, again primarily to architecture: this was the low-pitched gabled roof resting on a perpendicular pediment or tympanon at each end of the building. As early as the fifth century B.C. Pindar ascribes to the Corinthians the employment of this gable or pediment on a temple (XIII Olympian ode, 20 ff.). It is extremely probable that the Corinthian roof and the pediment were each conditioned by the other, for only thus could the Doric temple acquire its standard form. Similarly, the development of relief sculpture was probably also continually stimulated by the representations on the metopes and above all by those on the pediments themselves.

All these discoveries are clear symptoms of intellectual and cultural energy. One can only form a just view of Corinth and its position in the Archaic world when one realizes that it was the centre of the most active trade with the East and the parent of the most powerful colony in the West, Syracuse (founded in 734 B.C.). These facts also testify to the financial and economic power of the city and district of Corinth, and at the same time are to some extent almost a necessary precondition for them. In the sixth and fifth centuries, too, and indeed down to its capture by a Roman army in 146 B.C., Corinth was one of the richest and most powerful cities of Greece. Yet this later importance certainly did not approach, even remotely, the importance which Corinth must have possessed in the eighth and seventh centuries before Christ. To explain this phenomenon we must raise once again the question of the possibility and strength of oriental influence. We have already spoken of trade, but another link with the Near East is revealed as soon as one recalls that Corinth was the scene of the early appearance—and fairly lasting persistence—of a form of government whose origins lay in oriental principalities and satrapies, namely the tyranny.

Tyranny

The tyrant is something quite different from the 'kings' who in epic poetry, and especially in Hesiod, rule patriarchally over a peasant population. He sprang, it is true, from the nobility, but from the lower ranks of it, which originally did not play much part in government, and the function which he fulfils in political life is that of an autocrat who successfully opposes the aristocracy and deprives it of its rights. This is almost always effected by means of a *coup d'état*, in which the revolutionary relies on the support of the

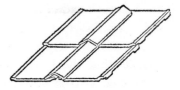

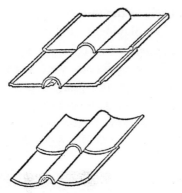

FIG. 7 – *Different kinds of Greek roof tiles: Lakonian, Sicilian and Corinthian (W. B. Dinsmoor, The Architecture of Ancient Greece, p. 44, Fig. 16).*

poorer section of the urban population, and if possible on that of a well-armed bodyguard. We are perfectly familiar with the process from the sixth century, and it is probably what happened in the seventh century too. Such tyrants first appear in the states on the isthmus, in Megara, Corinth and Sicyon. The most influential of them and indeed the founder of a dynasty was Kypselos of Corinth. His name is also inscribed in indelible letters in the history of Greek art, as that of the patron who commissioned various works of art and as a benefactor of the great mainland sanctuaries. He and his sons sent to Olympia and Delphi valuable votive gifts, which were still arousing admiration there centuries later. The chief of these was a statue or statuette of Zeus which—although less than life-size—was made of pure gold. We also know, but only from literary descriptions, of a box made of cedar wood artistically adorned with a host of mythological pictures. By good fortune one of these votive FIGS. 8–9 offerings, if only a rather more modest one, has actually been preserved. This is a gold cup of the sort customarily used for pouring libations. The cup's diameter is $6^7/_{10}$ inches and its weight 836 grammes; it is made of beaten gold and its delicate craftsmanship is amazing. The delicacy of the execution is matched by a sensitive feeling for artistic form. At first one is struck only by the simple plastic forms of the central circular base and the nine surrounding hollow sections; but closer inspection reveals the delicate double pearl ornament which, inside, forms the boundary

48

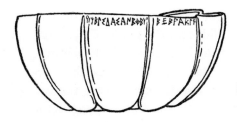

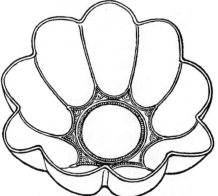

FIG. 8/9 – *Omphalos cup, votive of-
fering of the sons of Kypselos. Gold.
About 630 B.C. Diam. 6⁷/10 in.
Boston, Museum of Fine Arts (Bull.
Boston, XX, no. 122, 65–68).*

between the centre and these sections. Outside, round the lip, is
incised an inscription in correct Corinthian letters of the later
seventh century. The four words state that the cup was dedicated
by the Kypselidai, that is, the sons of Kypselos, out of (the spoils
from) Heraklea. It is true that the city of Heraklea, without any
further details, cannot now be accurately identified (it was probably
a town on the Ambracian Gulf); but for us the inscription makes the
vessel a historical document as well.

The continuity of this type of government, based on eastern models
and taking as it did the form of the monarchical régime of a usurper,
was undoubtedly responsible not only for the power and success
of Corinth in the early Archaic period but also for its artistic
efflorescence. True, it was only a precondition, not a cause. But
clearly in most cases tyrannies favoured cultural life rather than
restricted it. Even the huge quantity and high quality of Corinthian
clay vessels are due rather to the existence of the tyranny than to
the fact that there was, and still are, rich deposits of good clay in
the neighbourhood of Corinth. That the productiveness of the
Corinthians in technique and craftsmanship was not confined to
the ceramic industry has already become evident. The firmness of
their stylistic forms is reflected in sculpture too. The mouth of the
little perfume flask in the Louvre has already shown this, at any PLATE P. 46
rate in small-scale works. The proportions of the face on the perfume
flask bear a striking resemblance to those of a woman's head on a

PLATE P. 51 limestone relief from Mycenae. In both cases the outline of the face is similar. So are the cut of the eyelids and the shape of the nose; very similar, too, are the shapes of the lightly modelled eyebrows. In both faces the forehead ends in a horizontal line, and the hair-styles—the so-called 'layer wig'—are also identical. Thus the two heads cannot be very different in date and must also belong to the same artistic school, which in the case of the perfume flask has been identified through technique and material as the Corinthian school. It is no surprise that the relief too belongs to it. In the middle of the seventh century the enormous power of Corinth had no rival in the north-eastern Peloponnese. The neighbouring cities obviously recognized the primacy of Corinth just as much as the politically independent colonies did (though not always willingly), even when they lay as far from the mother-city as Corcyra and Syracuse. The distance between Mycenae and Corinth is little more than eighteen miles.

Relationship between sculpture and architecture

The relief shows that Corinthian sculptors were among the first who contributed to the sculptural adornment of Doric temples. It is very probable that the fragment formed part of a scene whose icono-graphic type persisted down to the mature classical period. On the fragment is depicted, under a horizontal ledge whose front edge has split off, the head of a youthful woman seen exactly full face. It is framed on each side by the abundant mass of long, horizontally grooved hair and at the top by little curls, which are represented by a double line of small circles. The figure was clothed in a tunic-like garment *(chiton)*, the upper edge of which is perceptible on the neck, and also in a big cloth or cloak which passed over the head and one corner of which, as the relief still shows, was pulled across in front of the breast, probably by the right hand. The movement of the left arm can also be deduced: obviously with the left hand the cloak was pulled far over to the right, for the triangle of shadow over the left temple is in the hollow made by the cloak, and is bordered below by the hair, but above by the edge of the cloak which is drawn almost horizontally to the right. The theme can only be explained as an unveiling. The figure is composed with a second figure in mind. If one compares the two-hundred-year later

Fragment of an architectural relief from Mycenae. Limestone. Third quarter of 7th century B.C. *Height 16 in. Athens, National Museum. Cf. pp. 50 ff.*

representation of the divine pair Zeus and Hera on one of the metopes of the temple of Hera at Selinus, and draws into the comparison the still more closely related group of the same pair of gods in the centre of the Parthenon frieze, the significance of the relief from Mycenae becomes certain. It is the same scene, represented here with simpler means, but no less impressively. The woman in the fragment of relief is a goddess and probably represents Hera.

The fragment belongs to a temple which was erected in the seventh century on the citadel of Mycenae. In the neighbourhood of this temple a bronze inscription was found which is about 150 years later than the relief and may possibly mention an Athena Polias. But it is by no means certain that this Athena was a goddess of Mycenae and still less certain that the temple on the citadel is a temple of Athena. It is not impossible that the temple to which the relief belonged was dedicated, like that at Selinus, to Hera: the Argolis and Samos are certainly the two original centres of the cult of Hera. On the other hand, the relief cannot have belonged to a series of standard metopes like the series on the Sicilian building. The relief from Mycenae was carved at a time when the standardization of the Doric order of architecture was not yet complete. Other fragments from Mycenae belonging to the same series of reliefs prove this; they cannot be described as genuine metopes. Thus the building, which we may guess from what we have said to have been a temple of Hera, must belong to a still proto-Doric phase in the development of architecture.

PLATE P. 54 Attempts have been made to see a stylistic connection between the relief from Mycenae and the goddess figure of unknown origin which, after being in a private collection, passed first into the museum at Auxerre and then, on loan, to the Louvre. Such a connection is by no means assured, although a stylistic relationship naturally exists. The 'Lady of Auxerre' has more frequently been regarded as Cretan; to judge by some of the details—the styling of the hair, the plasticity of the breasts, the ornamental pattern on the front of the chiton—one might perhaps also ascribe the origin of this figure to Samos or one of the Cyclades. However, the best place for it in our survey is here, for if it does not come from one and the same workshop as the relief from Mycenae it did come into being at the same point in the development of Greek art. And the figure as such can give us some indication of how we should visualize the whole figure of the Hera in the relief. The material of the two works—an amorphous, slightly yellowish limestone—is the same, too. The clothes are certainly different, and so is the hair-style. Over a patterned chiton pulled in by a broad belt the figure from Auxerre wears a short shoulder-cloak like a collar, as was the custom in Samos and Crete. The main arrangement of the hair to the left and right of the face consists in separate tufts of hair, divided vertically. Slight differences from the Mycenae relief can also be observed in the shape of the eyebrows and the detail of the eyelids. On the other hand, the total size of the figures is very similar: the figure from Auxerre is 2 feet 6 inches high; and as the fragment of the relief measures 17 inches from top to bottom the original size of the figures on the relief can be assumed to have been about 2 feet 4 inches.

Even if we were to ascribe the goddess in the Louvre to the Corinthian school, the north-eastern Peloponnese would still have no life-size free-standing statue to its credit. The forward-looking impulses, however, the main stream of development in sculpture, now flow from life-size, indeed larger than life-size and much larger than life-size statues. Few remains from this early period of the large-scale phase in Greek art have been preserved, but they are sufficient to enable us to reconstruct the original situation. The material used is mainly marble, which is now employed again by Greek sculptors for the first time since the Cycladic culture of the third millennium before Christ. Wood was certainly employed as well—the literary tradition testifies to this—and also wood covered with riveted bronze plates. The oldest life-size Greek statue that has come down to us is the marble statue of Artemis sent as a votive offering to Delos by the Naxian lady Nikandra. For this very precise information we are indebted to the statue itself, or, to be more accurate, to the inscription which the Naxian sculptor cut in delicate old-fashioned letters on the robe. The style and character of the letters make it possible to date this votive figure.

LARGE-SCALE
SCULPTURE

FIG. 10

Female figure from Auxerre. Limestone. Third quarter of 7th century B.C. *Height 2 ft. 6 in. Paris, Louvre. Cf. pp. 52 ff.*

It was carved in the middle, or shortly before the middle, of the seventh century. Next in order of time come some later statues, all of them more or less seriously damaged. The main sites where such statues have been found are Delos and Naxos. Further development was probably influenced by the rich natural supplies of good-quality marble in the Cyclades and by a certain tradition of crafts-manship which grew up particularly in Naxos and Paros. It was not until later in the seventh century that the tendency towards literal monumentality spread to other regions of Greece; the last areas to be affected were possibly the island of Rhodes in the east and the district of Corinth in the west.

In Rhodes, sculpture as a whole obviously does not play a very important part. All through the seventh century and on into the sixth one of the most characteristic products of the island's art is the series of vases decorated with friezes of animals—a very peaceful and harmonious kind of decoration, but also a somewhat prosaic one. The tapestry-like character of the decoration and the oriental floweriness and general feeling of the prototypes are here particu-larly well preserved. At Corinth the situation is quite different. We have seen that as early as the middle of the century the mythological picture was just as much at home, even on the little Corinthian oil-jugs, as were lively representations of scenes from contemporary life. Now old eastern pictorial schemes, such as the lion and bull fighting each other, are completely absorbed into Greek art and depicted with a dramatic force whose 'inner monumentality' is immediately striking. The technique of incising lines in the clay ground of the vase permits an effect otherwise restricted to the brazen sharpness of engraving in metal. What is genuinely ceramic, of course, is the scanty use of colours—white (now vanished, origi-nally on the lion's mane) and purple, in contrast to the dark surface of the vessel, to which the firing has given a greenish tinge.

The finest achievement of the whole Corinthian ceramic industry is somewhat later again than the jug bearing the picture just described. This masterpiece, also a jug, was formerly in the Chigi Collection and is now in the museum housed in the villa of the Renaissance pope, Julius II. It is $10^2/_5$ inches high and thus rela-

RHODES

PLATE P. 57

CORINTH

PLATE P. 59

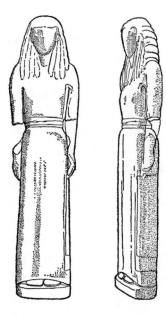

FIG. 10 – *Artemis, votive offering of the Naxian lady Nikandra. Marble. From the sanctuary of Artemis on Delos. About 660 B.C. Height 5 ft. 10 in. Athens, National Museum (F. Matz, Frühgriech. Kunst, I, Plate 78).*

tively big for a Corinthian vase. Yet its painter is unsurpassable in the miniature-like delicacy of his pictorial friezes. The top frieze shows a battle scene, but one in which the issue is no longer decided by individual duels between heroes, but by the clash of armies in close battle order. Below this is a narrow frieze in which hounds pursue fleeing mountain goats. The next frieze down, the second of the two main friezes, shows three quite independent scenes: chariots and a procession of horsemen, a lion hunt (these two pictures are separated by a heraldic sphinx), and, under the handle, the Judgement of Paris. Only in the last, the most badly damaged painting on the vase, has the painter inserted names—Alexandros, Athanaia, Aphrodite (and probably also) Hera and Hermes—by the corresponding figures, and thus defined them as characters from myth. From this we may probably deduce that the other figures are to be taken not as mythical characters but as persons from daily life—a life not only grounded in reality but also strongly tinged with fantasy. For it should not be assumed that lion hunts took place in the mountains of the Peloponnese at that time; it is much more likely that an Assyrian prototype has been adapted to Greek ideas and the Greek environment and then depicted with the nimble

PLATE ON TITLE-PAGE
PLATE P. 60

East Greek jug with friezes of animals. Second half of 7th century B.C. *Height 11³/₅ in.*
Boston, Museum of Fine Arts. Cf. p. 55.

agility of the Corinthian brush and especially the Corinthian stylus. The riders, together with their horses and the led horses, move with the same true Archaic boldness, but also with pride and grace. The more ancient hair-style of the 'layer wig' has been abandoned; instead, the hair is arranged in thick locks, which hang in front of and behind the shoulders. The wonderful wealth of tints which the firing has produced in the surface colours was certainly intended; they range from yellowish to light brown, from bright red to dark red and blackish russet. But perhaps the most curious thing about these pictures is the way they unconsciously live entirely in the present—their human, earthly quality. Although there can be no question of humour or even parody, there is a certain 'gaiety', a sort of earthy confidence about these scenes—about the lion hunt, which turns out badly for one of the participants and is indeed not without a touch of cruelty. These observations are particularly true of the bottom frieze, in which successful hunters wait behind bushes for the hares and foxes. The pictorial friezes are bounded at the top by a carefully incised band of palmettes and lotus on the mouth of the jug, and at the bottom by a zone of black varnish and the usual ray ornament on the ring of clay on which the vessel stands.

IVORY CARVING The ivory statuette of a kneeling youth found on Samos is contemporary and of equal, if not superior, artistic quality. But in contrast to the Corinthian jug it does not yet seem possible to ascribe it to a definite stylistic and regional school. Any attempt to

APPX. PLATES 2–3 attribute the ivory figure to the Corinthian school would meet various difficulties, although the hair-style is similar to that of the youths on the Chigi vase and the locks falling on to the front of each shoulder can confidently be called identical to those on the comparable pictures on the jug. The nimble precision with which the outline is executed is also perfectly comparable. But in ivory carvings that are certainly Corinthian the shape of the face is decidedly triangular, not so much rounded as in the statuette from Samos. This rounding, like the modelling of the lids and brows of the big eyes, is an Ionian feature. On the other hand, more or less contemporary Samian clay and metal heads do not provide completely convincing parallels. We must certainly take into account

Detail of a Protocorinthian jug from Veii. Third quarter of 7th century B.C. *Height of vessel 11¹/₅ in. Rome, Villa Giulia. Cf. pp. 55, 195.*

the fact that the business of the ivory-carver forced him to lead an unsettled, wandering life. He himself or his patrons had to procure the material for his work from distant India. In a description of the *Life of Apollonius of Tyana* (Philostratos, Ap. 5, 20), these words are put into the mouth of the philosopher: 'Earlier, in olden times, artists carried only their skill and their tools with them (the 'implements of the ivory-carver' are expressly mentioned), and executed

Lion hunt. Frieze on a Protocorinthian jug formerly in the Chigi Collection. Third quarter of 7th century B.C. *Height of vessel 10²/₅ in. Rome, Villa Giulia. Cf. p. 56.*

their commissions on the spot'. The traditions of this particular craft were certainly taken over by the Greeks from the Syrians, Phrygians and Phoenicians; it may even be that oriental artists travelled to Greece, then settled there and became hellenized. In any case, in comparison with Near Eastern and Phoenician ivory work the Samian statuette is completely Greek. From the technical point of view, it is true, especially in the technique of inlaying—the hair over the forehead, the brows, the eyes, the pubic hair—the artist is clearly a pupil of the experienced Syrian and Phoenician carvers. Even today there are still remnants of amber in the centre of the curls over the forehead. What distinguishes the statuette as a whole from anything oriental is the serene sobriety, the almost transparent clarity of its composition, its almost crystalline structure. This is all the more remarkable since it is not an autonomous work of art but part of an instrument of some kind. Various possibilities have been considered. The most likely one is that the youth, together with another similar figure, served as link between the sounding-board of a lyre and the revolving wooden rod on which the strings were stretched. The choice artistry of the ivory sections would not have suffered by insertion in a larger context; the whole instrument must originally have been of ethereal beauty.

FIG. 11

Thanks to fortunate and unexpected new discoveries, the early history of Greek free-standing sculpture is clearer than it used to be. So far as large statues are concerned, it has been particularly enriched by the excavations of the French on Delos, of the Greeks on Naxos, of the Germans in the Kerameikos quarter of Athens and of the Americans in the Agora. However, as we have seen, the mental attitude which leads to large-scale sculpture can also find expression in smaller works. From this point of view even small finds such as a wooden statue of Hera from the first half of the seventh century, or the ivory figure just discussed from the second half, are important for the history of sculpture. Both statuettes were discovered during the last few years in the sanctuary of Hera on Samos; they are now in the National Museum at Athens but are not on public display. In this connection a somewhat older find (1941) must certainly be mentioned: this is the bronze statuette of a charioteer which was dug up at Olympia in the immediate neighbourhood of the stadium. The pierced, clenched hands of this charioteer held the reins, and the right hand also held the guiding-stick. This figure, too, once belonged to a bigger whole; it formed part of a group consisting of horses, chariot and driver. Teams of this sort had been consecrated in the sanctuary of Olympia since Geometric times. But our statuette, preserved as it is in isolation, is distinguished by a special affinity with the chief type of Greek free-standing statue, known generally today as the *kouros*, a name which goes back to the Greek archaeologist Leonardos. The kouros

SCULPTURE IN STONE, WOOD AND BRONZE

PLATE P. 64

The kouros type

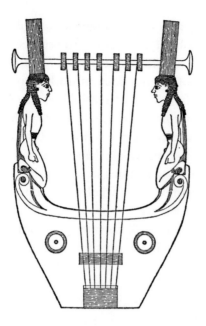

FIG. 11 – *Lyre from Samos. Reconstruction and drawing by D. Ohly (Ath. Mitt., 74, 1959, 54, Fig. 7).*

is a naked youth, standing, seen from the front and in all essentials presented symmetrically, with the left leg slightly advanced and the arms hanging down. This type, in all its hundreds of variations, can be regarded as representative of the whole Archaic art of Greece. In comparison, Geometric sculpture, in the proper sense of the term, for all its strong stylization, is in the last analysis less schematic: its proportions are not hard and fast; a fruitful conflict between naturalism and stylization can always be traced. In spite of this stylization Geometric sculpture as a whole shows less unity. Each separate statuette almost always displays a pronounced individuality in its detailed forms and sometimes even in its motive force. It is quite the opposite with the developed Archaic style. Variety and multiplicity are replaced by one single mathematically calculated conception—the type. Just as for Plato the world of appearances consists of reproductions, reflections of the Ideas, so every kouros statue seeks, as it were, to embody the idea of a kouros. It is true that, later on, variations of the type are permitted, and also that besides the kouros there are the types of the standing, clothed female figure and of the clothed sitting figure, but this does not affect the principle.

In fact Plato's theory of ideas and the formal types of Archaic art are related phenomena. But this does not mean that Archaic art is a sort of theory of ideas in concrete form anticipating Plato by centuries. In the first place, sculpture in Plato's time, and 'classical art' in general, with its tension between naturalism and stylization, is nearer to pre-Archaic art, to Geometric art; there is thus no question of tracing a constant development of the type towards the Platonic idea. In the second place, the Archaic types only acquire their real significance when one enquires of the outward forms what their inner meaning is, what sort of idea it is that they serve. This idea is completely un-Platonic.

There are numerous periods in history when the content of pictorial art is nature. This is true, in a general sense, of many lands and peoples, of many stages of development in the history of art. But this general statement covers all kinds of possibilities in the way of representation. So far as the mature Archaic art of the Greeks is concerned, the first and most important modification of the general principle consists in the fact that here nature is to be understood as directly perceptible by the senses, as tangibly present. Consequently the first characteristic of nature here is that it belongs to this world alone. This is also the sense in which we must take the description of the Greek philosophers of this period as natural philosophers. This is how we must understand Thales' conception, quite rightly described by Nietzsche as a brilliant revolutionary intellectual achievement, that *the origin of all things* was *water*. A philosophical maxim of this sort reflects, like the few basic types of archaic art, the unconscious, almost manic urge to go back to the simplest formulas, and above all to seek the primal matter, the beginnings, in the very simplest element. Moreover, this primal matter, this very simplest element, is not transcendent; it does not belong to the world of pure thought, to the realm of fable or mythology, but is in every sense a substance belonging to this world. When the philosopher Anaximander, the younger contemporary of

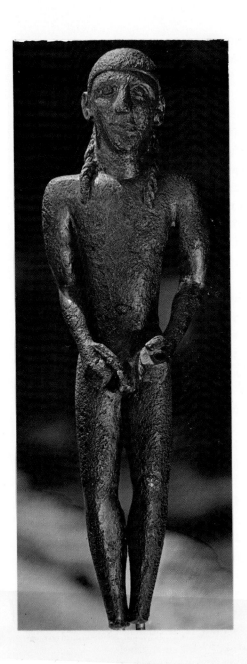

Thales, asserts that the 'infinite' is the origin of all things, his abandonment of this kind of material, substantial primal truth is only apparent. For it has long been recognized, and can be conclusively demonstrated from the fragments of Anaximander, that even this 'infinite' is meant to be something material, belonging to the physical world. In Anaximander, it is true, the extreme simplicity of Thales' views has been abandoned, and with it something of their grandeur. To Anaximander the infinite is not infinity itself but an infinite substance, from which an unlimited number of material creations is continually issuing 'by separation'; that is why the primal matter can be described as 'the infinite'.

Both Thales and Anaximander came from Miletos, the Greek city on the coast of Asia Minor. This prompts the question whether oriental influences were at work in the intellectual structure erected by these Ionian natural philosophers. The answer is that if their teachings owe anything to the East it can only have been the original impetus, which led to the most characteristic primitive Greek modes of thought.

Bronze statuette of a charioteer from Olympia. Second quarter of 7th century B.C. *Height 9¹/₅ in. Olympia Museum. Cf. pp. 61, 65.*

For the most important element in the early Greek philosophers' view of the world—and at the same time the unifying, common basis of both Thales' and Anaximander's views—is their extremely material character. This is paralleled in sculpture by 'the absolute representation of blooming, vigorous life through unnaturally simplified form'. That mind and movement, life and growth, exist only in physically tangible shape is such a typically Greek notion that it clearly remained valid down to Plato's day and basically down to the beginning of late antiquity in the third century after Christ. Sculpture goes a step further. At any rate in the Archaic period it is not nature as a whole in all its manifestations that is the main theme of art, but man himself. Implements and buildings, too, are seen in their relation to man. That even the shapes of vases and columns can be regarded as likenesses of the human form was noted long ago and has often been repeated. But these assumptions are particularly true of Archaic art: the statues radiate 'a sort of naïve, self-conscious pride in the beauty and perfection of one's own body and with it a joy in life far removed from any kind of reflection'. This is also an indication that in the Archaic period the identification of the human being with the statue may not have appeared impossible, at least in theory. Such an attitude, it is true, requires the statues to be at least 'natural size' or 'life-size'. Statuettes cannot be regarded in this light, however perfect of their kind they may be, like the bronze charioteer from Olympia or an ivory figure of a girl PLATE P. 64 from Ephesos. The statue of a youth in the Metropolitan Museum PLATE P. 67 in New York, on the other hand, seems, metaphorically speaking, like the very incarnation of a human being. APPX. PL. 4

We have already mentioned the marble fragments which testify to the existence of large-scale statues of the kouros type in the years following the middle of the seventh century. These statues show the human figure naked except for a hint of clothing in the shape of a belt. These belts, as a piece of clothing, are a tradition handed down from Mycenean times. In the seventh century they were worn by both men and women alike. Particularly valuable ones were made in Crete and the Near East from metal and leather, and were exported to all parts of Greece. It is dubious whether they formed a special part of the clothing of athletes. At any rate, the complete nudity which was finally adopted by the Greeks for statues of men is probably connected with a story which is told of some Olympic games held in the first half of the seventh century. Although this story is clearly anecdotal in character, it obviously mirrors changes in costume that actually took place and with them a change of attitude towards the human body in general. In the foot race, so the story goes, one of the runners lost his loin-cloth and as a result was the first to reach the finishing post; since then athletes had competed naked in the foot race. Two further conclusions can be drawn from this story. The first of these is that nude male statues and nakedness in athletic competitions can be regarded as having the same kind of significance and as being equally typical of Greek culture. The second is that nudity was by no means usual in daily life, even later on, and that even men appear naked only in sport and in the course of relaxed drinking-parties, as indeed is also proved by the multitude of vase-paintings. This means that nudity lifts the statue of a young man out of the ruck of his contemporaries in the same way as the athlete is elevated above everyday life in his moment of glory at festive games. The statue, too, is something festive. Its precise significance depends on where and for what reason it was erected, for it can be set up either in a sanctuary or on a grave. In the first case it represents a gift to the god, a dedication, which can be made either by a public body or a private individual. Thus the donor may be a community or, on the motion of the popular assembly, a city; but it can also be a more or less influential private citizen, a victorious athlete or his relatives, a general or captain, or finally the representative of any profession who would like to establish a favourable link between his life and activities on the one hand and the divinity on the other. The statue dedicated to the god can represent either this very divinity or the donor himself; but in many cases it can also have the general sense of a particularly beautiful and not precisely defined human being, of a perfect piece of sculpture.

If the statue is set up on a grave, it is not simply a monument to mark the spot; it also keeps alive the memory of the dead person buried there; it is—whether it is the statue of a man or a woman—a likeness. But this likeness is never physiognomically faithful and does not attempt to be. Sepulchral statues of men are removed from the world of everyday appearances by their nudity alone, as we have already seen. Although numerous inscriptions prove that people who died young were honoured by particularly splendid memorials, it is on the other hand just as certain that sometimes even the tomb of a man who died at a riper age was marked by a kouros statue, that is, by the statue of a youth. Thus these pieces of evidence can be used as proof that in life as well as in art the type was decisively preferred to the individual.

The youth in New York is the oldest fully preserved statue of the kouros type. This was a sepulchral statue; it stood originally in the burial ground of a family belonging to the Attic landed nobility. Relics of clothing are still present on this statue too, but they have even less to do with proper garments than the belt of the earlier phase; the neck band and hair band were only fashionable adornments. In the later

Statuette of a girl from Ephesos. Ivory. About 600 B.C. *Height* 2½ *in. Cambridge, Fitzwilliam Museum. Cf. p. 65.*

kouros of the sixth century the only one of these details that remains is the band that holds and orders the hair. It is there because it was part of the hair-style and could not be left out of the artistic reproduction of this style.

Another phenomenon in the development of Archaic sculpture must also be emphasized. It concerns the theme, in the simplest sense of the term. During the course of the phase that begins with the FIG. 10

APPX. PL. 4 votive statue of Nikandra and ends with the figure of the youth in New York, a thematic transformation is effected, in that at the start of this period a clear majority of the figures are female and at the end of it the majority are male. The following circumstance, too, gives the statue in New York a representative position in the history of art. In it for the first time, so far as we can see from the works that have been preserved, a Greek sculptor became aware of the possibility and master of the means of creating, in a freely stylized form, the large-scale free-standing statue of a man. And his personal signature is so characteristic that efforts could justifiably be made to recognize it again in a somewhat later work.

Both in our daily life and in contemporary art, we twentieth-century people start from very different premises and we must therefore be exceptionally cautious in any attempt to interpret in detail the general observations we have made about the statue in New York. From the purely artistic point of view, what we can say with some certainty is that here an Attic sculptor was enabled by superior creative ability to transform Cycladic models to suit a later age, and to bring them to life in such a way that one can speak, so far as the figure as a whole is concerned, of a 'new spring-like discovery of life' and, in connection with the countenance, even of 'an awakening of expression'. It has become equally clear, it is true, that many traces of tradition are still present; this is due mainly to the use of a type, which the sculptor found already in existence and which he passed on to his successors transformed and perfected. Besides bringing the forms to life, as we have already described, with results that are evident in every square inch of the statue's life-like surface, the artist was also responsible for injecting more volume into the figure, so that in spite of the crystal clear geometric structure of the four sides of the statue it seems much more three-dimensional than its older predecessors. The geometric arrangement of the surfaces on which the composition of the figure is based is most clearly evident in the stylization of the muscles and sinews, which are not by any means modelled naturalistically but with an eye to the formal articulation. Signs of these structures are already clearly discernible in the anatomical detail of the ivory youth from FIG. 11 Samos. In the youth in New York they are emphatically present in every view of the statue: on the back in the rounding of the shoulder-blades and elbows, at the sides in the modelling of the knuckles and calves, and finally from the front most clearly in the collar-bones, the lines of the groin and the knee-caps.

A black-figure amphora found at the port of Peiraieus more or less PLATE P. 70 corresponds in its shape, which is bulkier than that of earlier Attic vases, and also in the exceptional clarity with which the figures are drawn, to the stage of development in sculpture represented by the statue in New York. This shows that this statue, too, must be placed in the third quarter of the seventh century. In the total conception—in the relationship of the body of the vessel to the neck, and in the relationship of these two parts to the strong handles—the potter has achieved a unity of design similar to that achieved by the sculptor in the statue. But the artist who painted the vase still lags behind in this point. The forms in the pictures are thoroughly monumental and the black-figure technique, taken over shortly before and at first only with some hesitation, by Attic painters from the Corinthians, is now thoroughly understood and used for the whole of the decoration, but the individual elements of the pictures are thematically heterogeneous and do not combine convincingly, in the composition of the frieze, in a harmonious unity. Part of the reason for this is that the painter has been consistent and taken over from Corinth not only the technique but also some of the pictorial formulas which the Corinthian painters had worked out for their pictures. For example, the squatting lion painted under one of the handles of the amphora from the Peiraieus is an almost unmodified reproduction, both in its details and in its composition as a whole, of Corinthian models. Such formulas as

Sepulchral amphora from the Peiraieus. Third quarter of 7th century B.C.
Height 3 ft. 8 in. Athens, National Museum. Cf. pp. 69, 107, 160, 181.

these are alien intruders in the Attic stock of imagery. This is not very noticeable, to be sure, in the main picture, which shows two teams of two horses in echelon. Moreover, the way in which the horses are depicted again provides an excellent parallel with sculpture: here again Cycladic models are so independently transformed and adapted to the Attic style that the forms seem both more alive and clearer. Note the love and feeling for the proud creature's nature with which even the cock on the neck of the vase is painted. But the filling ornaments round the figures and the various bands of ornament above and below the pictures are not welded together into an artistic unity either among themselves or in relation to the pictures. In Athens complete harmony between all the pictorial and decorative elements and the shape of the vessel was not achieved until the next stage in the development of vase-painting.

Pausanias, the travel writer and mythologist of the imperial age, *Daidalos* says of the statues of a sculptor called Daidalos, some of which he had obviously seen with his own eyes, that they looked curious but had something divine about them. Other writers, headed by Plato (*Meno*, 97), emphasize—naturally in comparison and contrast with still older statues—the particularly life-like character of Daidalos' works. In them, say these writers, the limbs were not joined together as part of one block but freed from the body in such a way that one almost received the impression that the statues could move. Attempts have been made, certainly not without justification, to connect these traditions with the sculptor of the Archaic statue of a youth in New York. Now the name Daidalos is a professional name which several sculptors bore; it means roughly 'skilful artist'. Naturally these arguments are not sufficient to justify the hypothesis that the creator of the statue in New York was called Daidalos. But in this case the literary sources can help to illuminate the background against which the Greeks themselves saw such pieces of sculpture. Even if this artist still remains anonymous to us, we are at least lucky enough to possess in addition one of the masterpieces of his maturity, although in a very fragmentary condition. The head is preserved and it is a splendid one. In accordance with a PLATE P. 73

tendency already visible in the New York statue, the individual features have here been yet more completely emptied of any individual and accidental characteristics; they have been lifted into the world of eternity, into the realm of absolute and lastingly valid forms. For example, in the head and in the statue the wonderful ornamental ear is in each case the same and yet not the same: in the head the shape of the ear has been enriched and enlarged, both in its measurable dimensions and in the factors contributing to the now immaculate correspondence of each separate detail to every other. From the side, the main impression is that of the large surface area of the face; from the front, the most striking characteristic is the intellectually refined shaping of the slender skull with its deep-set eyes. The original height of the statue to which the head belonged was about 8 feet 4 inches, that is, about a third greater than the height of the statue in New York. The material is the same, namely Cycladic marble of the very finest quality. The head was found fifty years ago, during the excavations in the Kerameikos, built into the double gate (Dipylon) of the fortifications of Athens. Ten years later the right hand of the statue was found not far from the same spot, and forty years later five further fragments that probably belonged to it were discovered during the excavations in the ancient market-place (agora) of Athens. Parts of the left hand, right upper thigh and shoulders, parts of the back, the right knee and the left buttock muscle have been preserved in this way. But the breaks are so unfortunate that only three of these fragments fit on to each other. Nevertheless the structure of the figure as a whole can be visualized. It seems to have been still more slender than the statue in New York and very similar in outline. The fact that two of the fragments were discovered in the immediate neighbourhood of the great necropolis outside the gates of Athens suggests that the 'Dipylon statue' too was a funerary monument. If this interpretation is right, the memorial must have been a huge one; by this immense statue the likeness of the dead man would have been raised by the sculptor to the supra-personal level and turned into a sort of ideal norm. It has become usual to refer to this *Signature of artists* anonymous sculptor as the 'Dipylon Master'. However, the signature

Head of the statue of a youth from the necropolis outside the double gate of Athens. Marble. 620–610 B.C. *Height 17³/5 in. Athens, National Museum. Cf. pp. 71, 82.*

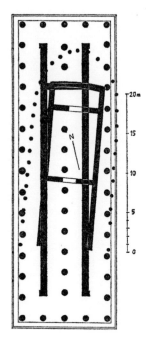

of a sculptor from the period of the Dipylon Master's maturity as an artist has actually been preserved on the base of a statue. This base was discovered on Delos and names one Euthykartides, who was not only the sculptor but also the donor of the statue which formerly stood on the base and of which the feet, legs and lower trunk are still preserved. The inscription raises the question of signatures in general. Although these signatures are certainly a measure of man's growing awareness of his individuality, and indeed, in the case in point, of his individual artistic personality, it is noteworthy that the oldest signatures known to us have by no means always preserved the names of the strongest and most independent artistic personalities, and that even later on, although artists certainly do frequently enough sign their works, they do not always do so and it is by no means always their best works that they sign. It is on vases that signatures first begin to appear but, characteristically, not on masterpieces of the important centres of production but rather in the hinterland of Greece or in the Italian colonies, that is, on the periphery; frequently the vases concerned are small and of relatively little artistic value. Most of the signatures date from the decades before and after 500 B.C. and are those of sculptors, potters and vase-painters. No inscriptions naming Greek builders or architects have come down to us; there are examples of these in Egyptian art, though in a slightly coded form.

Nevertheless, from the peak which we have now reached in the history of Greek sculpture, let us look—since we have already glanced at contemporary vase-painting—at the progress made in the meantime by architecture. At this point in time the historically important phases of architecture can best be followed in buildings belonging to the Doric order. In addition, it was precisely in Doric temples that sculpture and architecture began to form close links. For the laws of relief composition, as illustrated on metopes and pediments, partly determine and also fertilize the principles of

ARCHITECTURE

architectural construction. Finally, it is no accident that only in architecture did Corinthian art, whose delicate, miniature nature was described above, achieve large, monumental forms in its external dimensions, too. The painted metopes of Theron were created about 620 B.C. and the reliefs of the pediments in Corcyra about 590 B.C.

The temple of Apollo at Thermon has a long history and the remains FIG. 12 of the ground-plans of several versions have been preserved. In the oldest phase a princely house of the prehistoric period was obviously converted into a temple, and in a second phase a series of exterior supports, 'a garland of columns', was added, as in the case of the temple of Hera on Samos. But the decisive alteration occurred in the second half of the seventh century when a strictly symmetrical double-aisled temple was erected at Thermon, with a peristyle whose columns, in the proportion of 5 to 15, no longer stand on separate foundations but on one continuous foundation with a level covering course, the stylobate. The elongated, delicate proportions of the ground-plan can be directly compared with the slender form of the Dipylon kouros. Pretty well nothing is left of the walls and roof, but the shape of the ground-plan, the bottom diameter of the columns and the size of the intervals between the columns are enough to show that the columns themselves must have been exceptionally slender in their proportions. It may be assumed that wood was the material which dictated the manner of construction and the style of this building, although individual parts of it may have been made of stone—the capitals, for example, which probably projected a long way out over the columns, which were narrow in diameter at the top. Aetolia, the region in which Thermon lies, is very remote. In other parts of Greece wooden buildings had by this time already been superseded by stone ones, but the old-fashioned columns of Doric temples known to us at Delphi and in the Argolis show, with their slender elegance, that their shape was

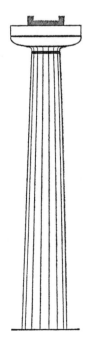

FIG. 13 – *Reconstructed column of the oldest temple of Athena Pronaia. Limestone. Second half of 7th century B.C. Delphi, Marmaria.*

75

originally conceived in wood. The same proportions can be assumed for the temple at Thermon, which was erected, to judge from the style of the metopes, about 620 B.C. These clay metopes are painted and fired by means of the same technique as Corinthian vases. The figures and ornaments, too, leave no room for doubt that they belong to the Corinthian school. What is striking is the monumental tranquillity of the mythological pictures. There is no attempt at graphic realism in the treatment. A gruesome legend is depicted PLATE P. 78 simply by putting the three main figures in fateful proximity to each other. It is true that originally these figures were also named; today most of the letters have perished and only one name, *Chelidon*,

FIG. 14 – *Reconstruction based on a model of a temple from Perachora. Terracotta. About 700 B.C. Athens, National Museum (H. Payne, Perachora, I, Plate 9b).*

←

FIG. 15 – *Prinias in Crete, Temple A. Second half of 7th century B.C. (Annuario della Scuola Arch. di Atene, I, 1914, 78, Fig. 43).* →

has been preserved. The version of the legend to which it belongs may have been current in Phocis, the region in which Delphi lies, too. Aëdon, the wife of Tereus, has killed her son Itys. By this deed, in which her sister Chelidon assisted her, the two women seek to take vengeance on Tereus, who had violated Chelidon and then torn out her tongue so that she could not accuse him. In spite of this Aëdon learns of the crime and of the criminal's name. The two sisters slice up the corpse of Itys and serve it to Tereus as a meal. Tereus kills himself and the two women are miraculously turned into a nightingale and a swallow. This is the legend which was told in very different forms in various parts of Greece and which was

Clay metope from the temple of Apollo at Thermon. About 620 B.C. Reconstructed. *Height about 3 ft. Athens, National Museum. Cf. pp. 76, 82, 87, 123.*

also used later by the tragic poets. The picture on the metope adopts a noble reserve in its treatment of this ghastly story. Between the women, on their knees, lies the corpse of Itys. On the original clay plaque the boy's upturned face can just be made out on Chelidon's lap. The well-preserved head of Chelidon shows even in the reproduction how simple, grand and monumental the picture's formal idiom is.

APPX. PL. 13

The temple at Thermon had a shallow ridged roof. Whether it had a pediment at each end cannot be determined for certain, but it seems probable that this standard form of the roof of a Doric temple had already been developed by the last few decades of the seventh century. The reader will recall the uncertainty which had to be admitted in connection with the roof of the Heraion of Samos. At the stage of development which we have reached now, all we can say for certain is that for the temple of Thermon a completely flat roof with a layer of earth on it can be ruled out as definitely as the steep roof displayed by little clay votive offerings in the shape of a temple which date from the late Geometric period. It is possible that this same kind of steep roof was used even in the seventh century for some temples of a curious design in Crete (Dreros and temple A at Prinias). We have already seen in another connection that seventh-century Crete, far from playing a particularly leading rôle, tended to preserve ancient traditional forms. Even if bold attempts were made there in architecture—in temple A at Prinias, in fact—to incorporate friezes in relief and even symmetrically arranged seated statues in the architectural unit, Crete certainly made no contribution to the development of the classical Ionic or Doric temple.

What is characteristic of the political scene all over Greece at this period is the emancipation of the nobility from its ties to the rest of the population and the concentration of power in the hands of relatively few men, a situation which not infrequently led to the emergence of a tyrant. Art, too, can only be understood when it is placed against this background. Something of this is reflected in the huge statues, whose proportions sometimes border on the realm of hubris. It is true that at this time, when tyrants ruled over many islands and in the Peloponnese, no tyrant had yet been successful in Athens. But this was not from lack of trying: constitutional history mentions the Athenian Kylon, who planned a *coup d'état* some time after 640 but came to grief. It is permissible to assume that the economic, political and military situation was fundamentally similar at that time in all the cities of Greece, no matter whether in one case a usurper had set up a tyranny or in another an influential aristocratic family or group held the reins of power. It is true of the bigger building enterprises at all periods that they

Relationship of art to politics

79

could only be carried through by the concentration of money and will-power at one single point. The best proof of this in the history of Greek architecture is provided by the great buildings of Ionian tyrants like Polykrates and by the building programme of Perikles. Such comprehensive and costly undertakings do not occur in the seventh century, but even then there are comparable examples, if only on a smaller scale.

III. RIPE ARCHAIC: EARLY PERIOD

(*circa* 620–550 B.C.)

If one wished to sum up in one word what the Archaic art of the Greeks still lacked after the revolutionary innovations of the seventh century and the great achievements of this period, especially the second half of it, one could perhaps use the word 'substance', substance in a wide sense, yet also one tailored to fit the particular historical situation. We do not mean by this—in sculpture, in the column, in the whole building—just the mass, the 'volume', which has already been mentioned now and again. Nor do we mean that in the seventh century artistic conceptions and their realization remained purely formal, that they lacked content and seriousness. The contrary is the case. What we mean to suggest is that it is only round about 600 B.C. that pictures, statues and temples acquire a certain weight, which certainly has something to do with material and mass but above all anchors the work of art firmly in the world of tangible bodies and through the complete correspondence of aim and execution lends it an expression of tranquil happiness. It is not until the sixth century that a pure harmony between form and content is established. Tensions which were really the essential element in the rhythm and composition of seventh-century creations are now fully resolved. It may be that this makes the individual artistic achievement less fascinating. The shock that one can feel at the realization of a seventh-century intuition will hardly be provoked by a painting or statue of the sixth century. Yet if one seeks to explain this phenomenon simply by the general statement that the age was a more civilized one, this assertion certainly contains part of the truth but by no means all of it.

Curiously enough this tranquillity can already be observed in a few works which belong to the middle of the seventh century and which in addition can almost be described as miniatures. From what *Animal figures* has been said already it can be guessed that the clay duck, a little PLATE P. 83 vase $3^2/_5$ inches long, in the Pergamon Museum in Berlin, belongs to the Corinthian school, and this is confirmed by the ornamentation and the quality of the clay. It is in fact the decisive nature of Corinthian forms and the plastic and intellectual substance of Corinthian art that were adduced to support their contention by those who wished to localize the origin of large-scale Greek sculpture in the north-eastern Peloponnese. As evidence against this hypothesis it has already been shown above that Corinthian art only acquires any correspondence between outward and inward greatness—and thus any monumentality—within the framework of architecture, and only at a point in time when the forms of the Doric order of architecture have also developed the monumental style, that is, when stone has replaced wood as building material. Two examples PLATE P. 78 were cited: the clay metopes of Thermon and the stone pediments of Corcyra. It only remains to take a closer look at these pediments. But first let us illustrate, by means of yet another example, the development that took place at Corinth from the small-scale phase of the duck vase to the large-scale phase of the Corcyra pediment. Here, too, it cannot be regarded as an accident that what we have called 'substance', the complete permeation of the plastic mass with creative form, appears first in quite simple but superbly observed figures of animals. Protocorinthian potters modelled ducks, owls, doves, hedgehogs and partridges, to name only some of the creatures that served as themes for plastic vases. They are all domestic animals, or at any rate animals that live in the neighbour-hood of man and are well known to him. What was found much more difficult, almost certainly as a result of psychological and religious inhibitions, was the creation of likenesses of man himself and of the demonic creatures supposed to be half man, half monster. This is why, to make an image of a man, a sphinx, a siren or a Centaur, an artist of the orientalizing age needed a certain super-abundance of creative power, of spiritual fire, the traces of which remained visible in the work of art when it was complete. This is the explanation of the mysterious, demonic violence reflected even in large-scale sculptures of the seventh century. It is thus quite under-standable that, before other parts of the kouros statue to which the PLATE P. 73 Dipylon head belongs were found, the head itself was taken for the

Protocorinthian oil-jar in the shape of a duck. About 650 B.C. *Length 3²/5 in. Berlin, Pergamon Museum. Cf. pp. 81, 115.*

head of one of these demonic creatures, for the head of a sphinx, in fact. The years around 600 B.C. bring a change in this respect. It is the change from the 'spiritual' form of the Dipylon kouros to the materially firm substance of the statues in Delphi—carved by an Argive sculptor—of Kleobis and Biton. It is this change that enables the tranquil, perfect form of the little duck, which is no PLATE ABOVE longer than a finger, to develop into the size—monumental for an animal figure—of a limestone lion in Corcyra. The massive, heavy animal, with its four-foot-long plinth, was originally set up on a PLATE P. 84

Limestone lion from a tomb in Corcyra. About 600 B.C. *Length of base 4 ft. Corcyra Museum. Cf. p. 83.*

tomb, or let into a big burial mound, in such a way that the edge of the base was not visible. The lion lay there like a mighty sentinel over the tomb. Its outlines, the stylization of the body, the thigh, the paw and a number of details about the head show, from comparison with vase-paintings, that the lion, too, is Corinthian. In fact it possesses precisely the qualities which struck us in older Corinthian works of art, now intensified by the large external dimensions. This enlargement may be partly due to the fact that the lion, too, was linked in a way to an architectural setting, namely to the man-made grave which it crowned. At any rate it is only from the stage of development attained by Corinthian sculpture in this figure that one can understand the importance of a large-scale pedimental relief which is a little later in date but still the oldest known to us.

The work in question is the relief at the back of the temple of Artemis in Corcyra, in other words the west pediment of this temple. Only relatively small fragments of the front pediment have been preserved; they show that its theme was the same as, or at any rate very similar to, that of the back pediment. The west pediment on the other hand is exceptionally well preserved, or at least completely enough to make the whole composition clear. The pediment is about eighty feet wide and consists of five sections similar in width but very different in theme. The parts that in content are oldest and richest in tradition are in the middle, where the shape of the pediment also gives them greater importance; the newer, more modern scenes are forced into the outer corners, or rather it is there that they appear, still in a very modest form, for the first time. The central scene is a large mythological picture. In it appears Medusa, one of those three demon sisters, the Gorgons. To the left and right of her are her children, the winged horse, Pegasos, and Chrysaor, who was human in form. According to the legend as it has come down to us in literature these twin children were born only at the moment of their mother's death. When Perseus beheaded Medusa with his sickle-like sword the twins came to life in the stream of blood that gushed up from the stump of the neck. In the relief the Gorgon's head still sits firmly on her shoulders. Perseus does not appear in this pediment. The artist is not trying to tell the story in pictures, so to speak; his aim is to show the terrifying face and all the terrifying attributes of demons—snakes, wings and the belt of knotted snakes. The children form part of this mythological picture and reinforce its character; they are shown on a much smaller scale, as further attributes of the central demonic figure.

Mythological pictures

Demonic powers similar to those of the central group are represented by the beasts of prey lying to left and right of it. In vase-paintings of the orientalizing period two main types of beast of prey were distinguished: one with the head in profile, often characterized by zoological details as a lion, and one with the head twisted round frontally which may rather be described as a panther. The animals on the pediment are of this latter type. But here the face shown frontally may have the additional task of reinforcing the terrifying, magically apotropaic character of the Gorgon. But why these apotropaic emblems on a temple? They follow an old tradition. Not only was the Gorgoneion, the fear-awakening and evil-averting power of the Gorgon mask, the petrifying stare of Medusa, affixed to shields, to Athena's aegis and to the walls of fortresses; the open

Head of a terracotta sphinx from Calydon. 580–570 B.C. *Athens, National Museum.*
Cf. pp. 88, 98.

end of the ridge beam of older temples was also obviously protected by a Gorgoneion. As the figure of the Gorgon on the pediment overlaps the frame of the pediment at the spot where the upward sloping cornices or *geisa* form an obtuse angle, here, too, the head stands in front of the open end of the ridge beam. There is no technical necessity for this; it is rather a case of traditional religious ideas being consciously taken over and embodied in a grand design. Finally, this design is also particularly meaningful because the Gorgon, like other divine and demonic beings, was conceived by the early Greeks as mistress of the animal world.

The scenes in the lower corners of the pediment reflect a different spirit and also spring from a different world in their themes. Here legends are related. The narrative, far more dramatically presented than the Itys saga on the metope of Thermon, also reflects different PLATE P. 78 aims on the part of the artists from those revealed by the central group. That was a would-be symbolic, heraldically composed excerpt from a myth; here, on the other hand, we find pleasure in events, pleasure in reporting events in a lively and clear fashion, and also joy in story-telling in its original sense. In the remainder *Narrative pictures* of the sixth century this joy in telling a story was to govern most mythological pictures. But on pedimental reliefs the distinction between the mythical-religious central figure and a saga unfolding round this central figure was still maintained for quite a long time. Even the epiphany of Apollo on the west pediment of the temple of Zeus at Olympia still clearly belongs typologically to this tradition. The pediment just discussed provides a second proof (the first being *'Monumentalization'* the metopes of Thermon) that in and with architecture Corinthian *of Corinthian art* art, at the end of a long process of development, attained monumental *forms* form as well. We can follow this process still further if we look at the temple of Artemis in Corcyra. But its significance is not restricted to Corinthian art alone; what Corinthian artists did for the modelling of animals, for pedimental compositions, for 'substance', for the lasting values of sculpture, extends in the course of the sixth century to the whole of Greece. On the other hand their work is also itself affected by influences from other sources, especially those emanating from the Attic tradition of sculpture. A notable example

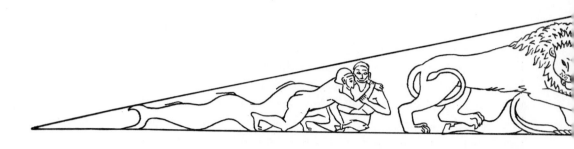

FIG. 16 – *Limestone pediment from the Acropolis, Athens. About 570 B.C.*

PLATE P. 86 of this is the sphinx of Calydon. Calydon, like Thermon, was an Aetolian town, and lay just as much in the sphere of influence of Corinthian art. The sphinx, made of terracotta, was used as a side akroterion on a ridged roof. Its physical lines, especially the modelling of the face, show the severe Corinthian structure. Only details like the shape of the shallowly carved, over-large eyes reveal *Attic influence* that Attic heads of the seventh century were known to the artist and that he chose their impressive 'spiritualization' as the model for his work. This is all the more noteworthy in that in the new century Athens herself did not remain equally true to her own principles. The reasons for this were political and economic factors connected with Solon's reforms, factors which naturally at first SOLON altered the image of the city in which Solon appeared, and indeed had to appear, on the scene because of the grievances which had built up in this agrarian state.

Solon was not the first reformer in Athens. A generation earlier Dracon had put the prevailing laws into writing and thus created a security guaranteed by law. The statutes drawn up certainly concerned serious crimes like murder and homicide, but other principles of law were also codified at that time. Even though constitutional decisions are supposed to have been included in Dracon's work, its importance lay primarily in reform of the law. *Nature and effect* But the social conditions that Dracon found in Attica demanded *of Solon's reforms* other reforms, too. They had become intolerable because when the small farmer incurred debts he fell into bondage and finally lost the ownership of his own land. This and other defects in the social

88

(*W. H. Schuchhardt, Archaische Giebelkompositionen, Fig. 3*).

structure could certainly be alleviated but not attacked at their roots by legal decrees. This was only made possible by the constitutional and legal reforms of the Attic nobleman Solon, who in 594 B.C. was chosen as arbitrator and invested with extremely comprehensive powers by the more or less organized political groups who were at loggerheads with each other. It is possible that social conditions in Attica were in a particularly unsatisfactory state. Already a hundred years earlier Sparta had democratized itself to an astonishing degree for an aristocratic state, by decreeing that the full legislative assembly of all Spartiates was to be convoked at least once a year. Yet it is significant for the leading rôle which Attica was to continue to play in the fields of culture and politics that the right man came forward to provide a remedy for the unhappy situation. One of the reasons for the lasting effectiveness of Solon's reforms was the simultaneous reorganization of the coinage and of weights and measures. This is also indirectly connected with the history of art in so far as Solon had the first four-drachma pieces with the picture of the owl struck at this time. But for the reform of the coinage and of weights, the further economic growth of Athens would never have taken place. The good quality of Attic products was only one of the preconditions for the world-wide trade which now began to develop; the other was the value, and also the easy exchangeability and computability, of Attic coins, which now conformed for the first time to the Euboean standard already introduced all over the Mediterranean world.

The abolition of slavery for debt, too, and the ensuing security of ownership for small farmers in the Attic agrarian state, was one further precondition of legislative and constitutional reform. This reform culminated in the re-organization of the population in four classes, arranged according to yearly income. These classes had different political rights and military duties. The privilege of birth was now replaced by the privilege of property. Fundamental as this change may appear at first sight, a good deal of tradition was preserved in the new organization, for the most lasting kind of property continued to be land. Thus if fundamentally Solon's constitution did not make the lowest into the highest, it did mean a tremendous strengthening of the structure of the state. In the fourth century B.C. Solon appeared to the Greeks themselves as one of the founders or forerunners of democracy, and there was some truth in this view. However, the tendency towards tyranny was not interrupted by Solon's constitution. In 582 B.C. a *coup d'état* established this form of government for the first time in Athens; it lasted for more than two years, but for no longer. The first man to achieve permanent success in this respect at Athens was Peisistratos, in 561 B.C. But first we must look at the time of Solon himself and the decades that followed his reforms. If Athens stands at the centre of developments in this epoch there is a good reason for this. In the field of ceramics it can be observed that almost all centres of production decline in output and finally stop production entirely during the course of the sixth century; the one exception is Attica. The only other areas with any kind of a reputation during the sixth century are Lakonia, which had several big potteries, and Chalcis. There is also a sharp decline in the importance of the East Greek potteries as a whole, in spite of some excellent isolated achievements. From the last decade but one of the sixth century onwards, Athens alone dominates the market. Demand from the chief export area, the cities of Etruria and central Italy, also seems to have been mainly for the products of Athens.

Another circumstance that helped to decide the pre-eminence of Athens in the cultural realm was the establishment of the festival of the Great Panathenaia, with its musical and gymnastic contests.

Pottery, vase-painting, sculpture and architecture remain monumental in style and retain the 'substance' that the Corinthians had conquered for Greek art. But in contrast to the slender, intellectually and geometrically ordered forms of the seventh century, Attic art in particular becomes, after and because of Solon's reform, more 'bourgeois'. The responsible class in the population has obviously grown considerably broader. In this connection it may be mentioned that the public exhibition of the texts of Solon's laws presupposes that most of the population of Athens could read. Understanding of the epic and lyric recitals at the Panathenaic festival was also probably widespread in the whole citizen body. New temples arose on the citadel of Athens at this time and the main temple of the goddess of the city was enlarged. A pediment of this temple can be reconstructed from the fragments that have been preserved. Comparison of it with the pediment from Corcyra reveals not only a toning down in all forms of expression but above all the greater importance that the legendary element has acquired in the composition as a whole. The pediment falls into three almost equally wide sections. The demonic element has disappeared from the central group. In a group showing animals fighting, the figures of the old animal frieze have been welded together into an action picture. Even in this central motif the later pediment has a more strongly narrative character. In the two outer sections of the pediment this tendency is completely predominant. On the left is a wrestling contest between Herakles and Triton, on the right probably the meeting between Zeus and Typhon, the snake-footed wind and fire demon; Zeus may have been depicted in the so-called 'kneeling-run' position, and only a small part of his cloak has been preserved, on the extreme left. In the present context it is the composition of the figure of Typhon that needs particular emphasis. The sculptor has given it three human bodies, which tail off into powerful, intertwined snakes. Each of the three bodies is equipped with a special attribute, held in each case in the left hand. Firebrand, wave of water and bird symbolize three realms in which Typhon is powerful. When one takes into account the earthy nature of snakes one is tempted to see here a pictorial representation of the

FIG. 16

PLATE P. 92

Figure with three bodies from a limestone pediment from the Acropolis. About 570 B.C. *Length about 11 ft. Athens, Acropolis Museum. Cf. pp. 91, 98, 175.*

four elements; however, there is no trace of a fourfold conception of the elements in contemporary natural science. The conquest of space and the capacity for psychological expression revealed in the three bodies and in their heads are more important. In contrast to the strictly orthogonal arrangement of the axes of movement in older Archaic art, here we meet for the first time, in the head furthest to the right, the three-quarter view. It has been claimed that the expression of different temperaments can be discerned even in the heads of the two beasts of prey on the pediment from Corcyra, but in the pediment from the Acropolis the sharp differentiation in facial expression of the three heads of Typhon is quite obvious. The differences in characterization are underlined by the colours of the paint employed. The remains of colours on the amorphous, relatively soft limestone provide some idea of the way in which Greek sculpture of this period was painted. The sculptor has made a special effort to give the eyes an expressive look by plastic modelling of the iris and pupil. Pieces of sculpture like the one just described suggest the thought that at this stage of its development Archaic art was in a position to create the spatial link between one figure and another, and a rhythmically governed relationship between figure and space. We certainly see a tendency in this direction inside the pedimental frame formed by the geisa. In free-standing sculpture such a form of composition, if it involved two or more figures, would result in what is known as a 'statuary group'. But since the compositional principle of Archaic art always consists in putting the separate component parts alongside each other and letting them stand on their own merits—a principle of composition usually known as 'additive' or 'paratactical'—there is no tendency at all towards the creation of real groups. Instead, statues are placed in rows. To make the acquaintance of the finest extant example of this we must leave Athens for the other centre of mature Archaic sculpture, the island of Samos.

There, about 560 B.C., a donor erected in the sanctuary of Hera a *Samian sculpture* long base on which six marble statues stood side by side. Four FIG. 17 standing figures, of which the one on the far left was probably a youth in a cloak, were framed on the right by a recumbent figure and on the left by a sitting one. All the figures had names inscribed on them. The artist, Geneleos by name, also inscribed his own GENELEOS name. Four of the figures are complete except for the heads, which were probably knocked off on purpose in medieval times. Fragments of a fifth, the third standing maiden, have been preserved. The statue of the youth has so far not come to light in the excavations. Even lined up alongside each other as they are today, the statues form a highly impressive monument. But the execution of each individual figure is unsurpassable. The statue of Ornithe can serve PLATE P. 96 as an example. The special delicacy of the surface texture lies in the

quite shallow modelling and the tender, tranquil play of the folds of drapery. The beauty of the girl herself, the delicacy and costliness of the garment are rendered by the artist by means of the thick hair cascading far down the back and the four simply arranged locks falling in front between shoulders and breasts, and also by means of the contrast between the somewhat more deeply carved narrow folds on the upper part of the body and the broader and rather shallower ones of the lower part. The garment is brought to life by the quiet gesture of the right hand lightly catching up the material.

Another, possibly still more important, sculptor must have been at work in Samos at that time; it was he who made, among other things, the splendid statue of a woman which, according to the inscription on it, was dedicated to Hera by one Cheramyes and is now in the Louvre. In spite of the difference between the two sculptors' artistic signatures the single figure reflects just as clearly as the group of statues by Geneleos the characteristic basic structure of East Ionian, and in particular of Samian, sculpture. Not only Attic structure but also that of the Cyclades can be easily distinguished from Samian. When in the eighties of the last century the excavations on the Athenian Acropolis brought to light for the first time monuments of Archaic art in unexpected abundance, the statues of maidens (korai) were regarded as the most remarkable of the finds. There are three dozen of them; the smallest are half life-size and the biggest is over eight feet tall. After initial amazement at their supposedly stiff schematic style it was gradually recognized that underneath the symmetrical forms the flourishing life of the Archaic period was not repressed but simply contained. This is the impression received by the writer Hugo von Hofmannsthal: 'There were statues there, female statues, in long robes. They stood round me in a semi-circle. In their perfect tranquillity, filled to the brim with life, they seemed to look down or into the middle distance, but they did not see me. Yet they were not unseeing; this impression may have sprung from the wonderful life with which the eyelids were endowed and which flowed in towards the root of the nose and was lost in a sublime seriousness under the eyes.'

Ionian and Attic korai

Stylistic comparison with similar statues from other sites in Greece shows that more than half the korai found on the Acropolis are the work of Attic sculptors. As for those which are certainly imports, the provenance of some can be stated with a considerable degree of probability. But the chief fact to emerge is that this type of statue was at home in Ionia and migrated from there to Attica. Statues like that of Ornithe were the prototypes which inspired the sculptors of the other regions of Greece to produce similar works. The clothing alone would show that Ionia was the source of these figures. There the oldest of them are dressed in the chiton, a tunic-like garment made of thin, delicate material. Later on, parts of this garment are pulled up high on both sides of the body, over the belt. The belt still remains visible, both in front and behind, between the resulting rolls of material, which hang down in fine folds, as on the statue of Ornithe. In some cases the belt is completely hidden by the roll of material, which is pulled down low. This style of dress can be enriched by adding to the chiton a short cloak, which is usually fastened on the right shoulder. In Athens the chiton was adopted in place of the firmer and thicker sleeveless garment usually worn previously in Attica, and later on the small, slanting

PLATE P. 96

cloak was taken over as well. Ionia was thus the model where fashion was concerned. The oldest korai dedicated on the Acropolis are the work of Ionian sculptors. The attempt to fix their place of origin pointed to Samos or one of the Cyclades. Today it can be said that the figure preserved complete with head, and holding a FIG. 18 fruit as an attribute, must be Naxian. The rhythmical treatment of the surface is so different from the lightly stirred surface of the statue of Ornithe that an ascription to a Samian sculptor is out of the question. The Naxian figure is also more angular, and the ridges of the folds in her clothing are just a little harder than the lines incised in the clothing of Samian statues. It has been said that Naxian bodies are lean, 'as though consumed by the sea wind'; this is perfectly true of the statue on the Acropolis. Of course, we do not know whether it was imported as a finished article or carved in Athens by a Naxian sculptor from a block of good island marble; both possibilities are equally likely. In comparison, the softer manner of Samian sculptors, with their habit of modelling the surface more strongly, is displayed by a curious votive offering, again from the sanctuary of Hera on Samos. It is a man about to FIG. 19 make a sacrifice and leading a cow to the goddess. Only fragments have been preserved. With the help of the pieces of the base and especially of the man's hand, which is grasping the cow by the horn and leading it, the relative positions of animal and man can be reconstructed. Here, too, there was no intention of creating a group in the later sense of the term. The cow and the man leading it are both walking in the same direction; both figures are stretched, as it were, in one orthogonal framework. Although the composition is certainly not naturalistic the mutual relationship of the figures seems full of life and the skin of the marble surface seems almost to breathe, even in the fragments of the badly damaged monument. Compared with Attic sculptures, Ornithe, the man leading the cow and the Naxian maiden in Athens naturally fall into a closely

Ornithe. Marble statue from the votive group by the sculptor Geneleos in the Heraion of Samos. About 560 B.C. *Height 5 ft. 6 in. Berlin, Pergamon Museum. Cf. pp. 93, 95, 133.*

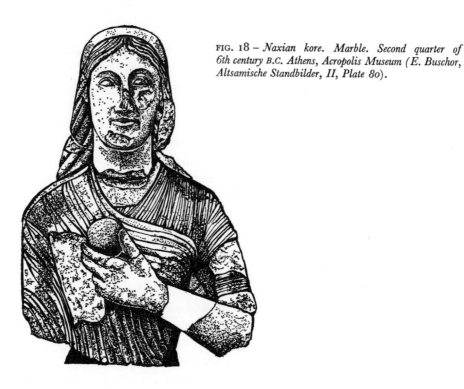

FIG. 18 – *Naxian kore. Marble. Second quarter of 6th century B.C. Athens, Acropolis Museum (E. Buschor, Altsamische Standbilder, II, Plate 80).*

related, if not absolutely homogeneous, stylistic group. Attic artists are concerned less with questions of the articulation of the surface and the modelling of the marble skin than—and here they are closer to the sculptors of the Peloponnese—with the way in which the separate parts of the body fit together and the relationship of these to space. This approach becomes more and more pronounced as Archaic form develops in the course of the sixth century. The

PLATE P. 92 triple-bodied creature from the pediment of the old temple of Athena was a good example. It continued the stimuli provided by Corinth. Its relationship to the pediment of the temple of Artemis in

PLATE P. 86
FIG. 20 Corcyra is repeated in that between the sphinx of Calydon and a sphinx which came to light in the cemetery area of the Kerameikos at Athens. Here the later work is distinguished from its older predecessor not by stronger spatiality or an attempt at a composition with a three-quarter face, but by the stronger articulation of the face and of the animal's body, together with a stronger sense of

movement in the, so to speak, momentary attitude of the whole figure.

The sphinx from the Kerameikos is also clearly later from a stylistic point of view than the Naxian and Samian sculptures just discussed. It leads on to a statue that can certainly be described as a masterpiece from the early period of the tyrant Peisistratos. Thanks to a young archaeologist's amazing memory for forms, a successful attempt was made thirty years ago to link the fragments of a horse and its rider in the Acropolis Museum at Athens with a marble head in the Louvre whose origin had long been unknown (for the Rampin private collection was only an intermediate stage on this head's fateful journey). Humfry Payne remembered in Athens the broken surface which he had seen in the Louvre, and a trial with a plaster cast showed that the Rampin head fits exactly on to the torso of the horseman in the Acropolis Museum. This brilliant feat made possible the reconstruction of the whole statue, at any rate on paper or in plaster, a statue that unites tendencies towards a conquest of space with the more vital and more strongly organic modelling of the parts of the body. Here an Attic sculptor drew the logical conclusions from the premises bequeathed to him by his older contemporaries in the shape of the limestone pediment and the marble sphinx.

Attic sculpture in the time of Peisistratos

PLATE P. 102

FIG. 21

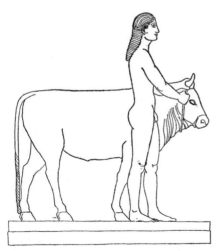

FIG. 19 – *Man leading a cow. Marble. About 560–550 B.C. Samos, Heraion (reconstruction by K.-F. Krösser).*

FIG. 20 – *Sphinx from an Attic tombstone. Marble. About 560 B.C. Athens, Kerameikos Museum (D. Ohly in 'Neue Deutsche Ausgrabungen', p. 254).*

However, study of the equestrian statue did not come to a halt with the successful matching of the head and the torso. Further examination of the marble fragments uncovered in the course of the excavations on the Acropolis led to the discovery of the remains of a second equestrian statue similar in style but facing in the opposite direction. The fragments are so scanty and in such a poor state of preservation that a reconstruction is impossible. However, the existence of a second statue forming a symmetrical counterpart to the first is quite certain. We are thus confronted with a double monument, consisting of two short-bearded horsemen, which it is not easy to explain. Because of the apparently individual treatment of the features the suggestion was once ventured that the statues were possibly intended to be portraits. People even thought they might be portraits of Peisistratos' two sons, who succeeded him in

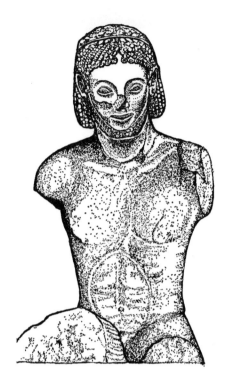

FIG. 21 – *Equestrian statue from Athens. Marble (head in Paris, Louvre, torso in Athens, Acropolis Museum). About 550 B.C. (H. Payne, Archaic Marble Sculptures from the Acropolis, Plate 11a).*

power after his death. In this case we do not need to broach the difficult question how far the possibility of individual characterization goes in named statues of men in the sixth century. At the time when the statues were carved Peisistratos' sons were certainly still too young to be represented by this type of figure. The suggestion that they represent the Dioskouroi may be nearer the truth. Yet no other dedications to Helen's brothers have been found on the Acropolis, nor have any inscriptions referring to them. There are numerous reliefs celebrating the two brothers in Sparta; such a monumental votive offering would fit in better there than on the citadel of Athens. All that is certain is that the Rampin head is purely Attic, as is shown by a comparison with the head of the sphinx from the Kerameikos. It is probably even possible to ascribe still further statues from the Acropolis material to the 'Rampin

Head of a horseman. Marble. 560–550 B.C. *Height 8 in. Paris, Louvre. Cf. p. 99.*

Master', and Payne tried to do this. But the fragment of a grave PLATE P. 104 relief of about the same time is much closer to the Rampin head from the stylistic point of view. The man depicted here holds a discus behind his head with his raised left hand, so that the face, bordered by the outside edge of the disc, appears in a kind of round frame. In this relief the sculptor has been wonderfully successful in conveying the delicate transitions from one surface of the face to another and the precise modelling of the bones of the skull underneath the taut skin. The athlete's hair-style resembles that of the Dipylon head in that the hair is tied together on the nape of the neck, though it is no longer arranged in so-called 'bead ringlets' but only divided horizontally. It is extremely probable that at the court of Peisistratos, as later at that of his sons and at the court of PEISISTRATOS Polykrates, there were sculptors and other artists as well as poets. At any rate the delicacy of the craftsmanship in both the Rampin head and the discus-bearer is thoroughly understandable in the context of court patronage of the arts. The relief proves that Athens was still the leader not only in votive statues, such splendid examples of which have been preserved on the Acropolis, but also in the art of funerary monuments. In the sixth century the grave is usually no longer marked by a vase or a free-standing statue but by a slab bearing a relief. Attic sculptors began to develop these grave reliefs *Attic grave stelai* from about 570 B.C. onwards and during the course of the next two and a half centuries they brought them to perfection. These 'stelai' are not really cheaper or more modest monuments; they often surpass funerary statues in size. This is true at any rate of the earliest phases of the development, when the stelai are also sometimes so thick that they assume the character of a pillar. They are frequently crowned with a capital, which also serves as a base for a figure or a floral akroterion. Later, in the time of the Athenian democracy, the mass of the population—and hence the authorities— more than once came to regard the splendour, luxury and size of these funerary reliefs as so offensive that decrees were passed forbidding costly funerals. But there was no question of this in the time of the aristocratic régime before Peisistratos or in the time of the tyranny. In those days the tall, narrow stelai were usually

Discus-bearer: fragment of a grave relief. Marble. 560–550 B.C. *Height 13 in. Athens, National Museum.* *Cf. p. 103.*

adorned with only one figure. It represents the deceased, whose memory is kept alive on earth by it. The figure on a stele is usually naked, but it can also be depicted clothed or armed. Younger men are very frequently shown with sporting gear. In general, this form of memorial in Attica seems to have been reserved for men. But exceptions and also extensions of it are known. For example, in one case a youth is accompanied by his sister, who is depicted on a much smaller scale. Pictures of mother and child are attested even for the Archaic period. But these are isolated forerunners of those 'family reliefs' which only became usual in Attica after the interval following the first prohibition of too costly tombs, in other words in the classical period. These later grave reliefs tend to be wide instead of tall, and two, three or, on occasion, even more figures appear on them.

The relations of the tyrant and his family with the potters and armourers were certainly not so close as their relations with the creators of large-scale works of art. Yet these branches of art or arts and crafts also flourished with particular vigour in Athens at that time. We can best appreciate the special character of Attic vase decoration by looking first at work that is in complete contrast to it, namely two vases from Lakonian workshops. These are the LAKONIAN VASE-PAINTING only workshops whose average products attain the level of Athenian ceramics in the sixth century. One of these vases is a big mixing vessel, in which wine was mixed with several parts of water, as APPX. PL. 12 was usual at feasts. To emphasize the sturdy shape of the vessel the painter has not used a figure picture or a frieze. Instead the decoration of this splendid vase consists of big ornamental designs, whose precision is reminiscent of metal engraving. Ever since the Geometric age figures had shown a tendency to acquire independent significance and to endanger, if not destroy, the unity of the vase as a whole. So long as the Lakonian painter confines himself to a variety of powerful ornaments, which correspond in every detail to the tectonic structure built up by the potter, he escapes this danger. With the Attic painter one almost gets the impression that he is deliberately seeking it. It is different with the decoration of the numerically largest category of Lakonian ware, drinking-cups. Only a few of these carry purely ornamental decorations; most of them are adorned with figure pictures, frequently only on the inside, so that—covered by the wine—they develop a curiously magical kind of life for the eye of the drinker. A good example of this is provided by a cup in the British Museum with a picture of a horseman in it. APPX. PL. 15 The treatment of the rider, the various birds—vultures and eagles— and especially the winged figure behind him carrying garlands, show that the rider is conceived as a hero. This is probably also the significance of the floral ornament growing up out of the volutes

FIG. 22 – *Lakonian cup. About 550 B.C. London, British Museum (R. M. Cook, Greek Painted Pottery, Plate 27b).*

which he carries on his head. Pictures of this sort lead to the assumption that some of these Lakonian drinking-cups were not only intended for normal use but were also conceived from the start as accessories for tombs.

FIG. 22 A surprise awaits us when we look at the vase from the side, and the same surprise must have been felt by the users when they first laid eyes on cups of this particular shape. Since the Geometric period shallow drinking vessels had been equipped with a short foot or just a circular ridge, on which they rest firmly when they are put down. The new kind of long-stemmed cup was invented in Sparta and it can be confidently asserted that no change of shape in the history of Greek vases gave a vessel such a different appearance in ponderation and tectonic as this new creation. The effect of this discovery was consequently a lasting one. Naturally it too underwent modification in the living, creative process of Greek pottery manufacture. Yet but for its Lakonian predecessors that category of cups which may perhaps be regarded as the climax of Greek ceramics, the Attic red-figure cups of the decades after 500 B.C., would never have been produced. The possibilities inherent in the relationship of the handles to the body of the cup, and of the lip of the cup to the tall stem, which grew more and more slender as time went on, are endless.

Most Lakonian cups are painted on the outside with purely ornamental designs. Round the spot where the stem meets the cup there are concentric circles, lines of pomegranates, leaf patterns

and other simple ornaments. Higher up, special attention is given
to the ornamentation of the handles. A very simple but effective
mode of decorating the lip of the cup is to leave it unpainted, so
that we see the finely-puddled, light slip which serves as the surface
for the paint on all Lakonian and East Greek vases. Other forms of
decoration found on the lip are patterns of leaves, blossoms, buds
or pomegranates; they emphasize the ribbon-like character of this
part of the vase, which widens out to the edge and is sometimes
slightly convex.

The Lakonian cup with the horseman probably dates from about *Attic vase-painting*
the middle of the sixth century. Attic vases of the same period are
totally different in character. They are also more representative
of the art forms prevalent at that time in Greece as a whole. Just
as some eighty years earlier the Corinthian jug in the Chigi Collection could be regarded as representative of that particular phase in
the history of Greek ceramics, so the krater made about 560 B.C.
and now in the Archaeological Museum of Florence is a typical   PLATE PP. 108–9
example of its own epoch. The centre of gravity has clearly shifted   PLATE P. 111
from Corinth to Athens. The krater is signed by the painter Kleitias   KLEITIAS
(or Klitias) and the potter Ergotimos. What is curious is that the
small forms that we observed in the seventh century at Corinth
now begin to prevail in Attic vase-painting. This may be connected
with the historical law that in any line of development a particular
phenomenon is often succeeded by its exact opposite. We made the
acquaintance of monumental forms in Attic vase-painting of the   PLATE P. 70
second half of the seventh century. They are developed further by
two—for us—anonymous painters of the turn of the century, the
Nessos painter and the Gorgon painter. However, in the late works
of the Gorgon painter there are already signs of this other tendency
which reaches its climax round the middle of the sixth century in the
miniature pictures of some Attic cup-painters appropriately known
as 'Little Masters'. The vase-painter Kleitias brought his small
forms to perfection on big surfaces and on a vase of above average
height. This was only made possible by a minute division of the
total area available. Kleitias opted for a division of the surface into
six horizontal strips. All these friezes are filled with figures; orna-

Calydonian boar hunt. Chariot race at the funeral games in honour
of Patroklos. Pictures on the neck of a volute krater bearing the

signatures of Kleitias and Ergotimos. 570–560 B.C. *Height of vase 2 ft. 2 in. Florence, Archaeological Museum. Cf. pp. 107, 110.*

mental decoration plays only a small part in comparison. The main frieze, on a level with the lower attachment of the two handles, depicts the visit of the Olympian gods and other divine and semi-divine figures to the newly-wedded couple Peleus and Thetis. On the lip of the vase—on one side—a story from the earlier youth of Peleus is told, the hunting of the Calydonian boar. Peleus takes part in the adventure as well as Meleager and Atalanta. The boar is the central figure in the composition of the frieze. It has already laid low one of the hunters and one of the hounds, but the others press forward indefatigably from right and left. Peleus and Meleager occupy the decisive, and at the same time the most dangerous, position in the circle of huntsmen. They hold their short spears in the way prescribed by ancient hunting rules—and still employed in the classical western boar hunt—for killing the wild boar: they approach the animal head on, guiding the 'hog spear' with the left hand and holding it firmly in the right.

Kleitias' originality lies in a programmatic arrangement of the pictorial friezes in such a way that the separate themes echo each other. Two other main themes stand out besides the Peleus myth. On the front of the krater Greece as a whole, so to speak, is celebrated in epic pictures of legends whose hero is Achilles. These are closely linked to the Peleus myth in content. The marriage of Peleus and Thetis forms the prelude to the legends about Achilles, for he was the son of these two. Thus it is not without point that themes from the story of Achilles are treated above the beginning of the procession of gods and also below it. Below is the pursuit of the Trojan prince Troilos by the fleet-footed hero, and on the neck of the krater the funeral games arranged by Achilles after the death PLATE PP. 108–9 of Patroklos: we are shown a scene from the chariot race in which Diomedes, Automedon and others participated.

The back of the vase is devoted to the celebration of Theseus. He corresponds here, as the native hero of Athens, to the hero of all Greece whose story is told on the front. On the lip of the vessel we find the joyful round dances performed by Theseus and Ariadne PLATE P. 111 after their escape from the palace of the Minotaur and underneath this, on the neck of the vase, battles with Centaurs, in which Theseus

Battle with Centaurs. Picture on the other side of the neck of the krater signed by Kleitias. 570–560 B.C. *Height of vase 2 ft. 2 in. Florence, Archaeological Museum. Cf. pp. 107, 110.*

is again involved. This last theme shows in one example the comradeship in arms between the Thessalian prince Peirithoos and the youthful Attic hero—and later king—Theseus. In the period that follows it is a favourite theme for the reliefs on Greek temples. While all the pictures so far mentioned are full of epic seriousness, the frieze of figures which rounds off all the cycles of pictures and is painted on the conical foot of the vase shows distinct traces of humour. Here we find the theme of the Pygmies' battle with the cranes. We shall have occasion to return to this subject in connection with the vase-painter Nearchos.

When these pictures are compared with those on the older Corinthian jug the stylistic differences become clear. These are explained first by the difference in date, then by the different regional styles

of Corinth and Athens, and finally by the different temperaments of the two painters. Although the Corinthian was working at the height, if not yet quite in the final stage, of a long process of artistic development, he draws in a much more naive way. Kleitias draws carefully, earnestly, industriously, and for that reason his figures are sometimes a little stiff and academic; yet they can move convincingly in many different ways, ranging from majestic dignity to slender elegance, according to the theme of the picture. One detail that is not unimportant for the style of this period should be mentioned. By this stage the relationship of art to reality has changed so radically in comparison with the Geometric age that, to take one example, conclusions can be drawn from vase-paintings about the weapons used at this time. The helmet worn by the Lapith Hoplon—just by giving him this name Kleitias introduces him as a representative of the heavily-armed soldiers of those days— corresponds even in its details to a helmet of the same period found at Olympia. Of course, some of the details can be recognized more clearly in the actual helmet—such things as the ornamental silver nails over the eye-slit and on the cheek-pieces, which the vase-painter has indicated by a double line. But the shape is similar, and the same is true of shield and armour. The best surviving example of Archaic armour, likewise from the excavations at Olympia, and so well preserved that the shimmering bronze has retained its elasticity until today, belongs to the time of Kleitias. Kleitias is the second oldest Attic painter whose name has been preserved for us by his signatures. The first, Sophilos, may have been the teacher of this gifted pupil. In several cases we can clearly prove Kleitias' dependence on Sophilos. In none of them has Kleitias has slavishly copied his model; he introduces variants into the individual sections of the pictures and, above all, he writes his own artistic hand. Thus he has taken the procession of guests at Peleus' marriage, the chariot race after the death of Patroklos and the picture of the fight with the Centaurs from older pictures by

FIG. 23 – *Shield handle from Noicattaro. Bronze. About 560 B.C. Bari, Museum (Gervasio, Bronzi arcaici, Plate 17, left). Cf. Appx. plates 6, 7, 9.*

Sophilos and painted them in his own style. In another respect, too, Kleitias continues a custom started by the older painter: neither Sophilos nor Kleitias leaves us in any doubt about the content of his pictures. Almost every single figure is named, even horses and dogs; indeed, even an altar or a water-jug has its name written alongside it. Obviously these inscriptions have a formal, decorative function as well as a thematic one.

With these pictures and their signatures, with the relationship of the individual painters to one another, we are already in the midst of the life and bustle of the potters' quarter in Archaic Athens. Sophilos had modelled, painted and fired his vases himself. Kleitias and Ergotimos seem to have joined forces to run a sort of firm, in which the former worked as master painter and the latter as master potter. But this division of the work was by no means the invariable rule from then onwards. For example, the somewhat younger Nearchos, a man who became wealthy as well as famous through his art, painted the vessels he had made himself. A dependent relationship in the matter of themes, of the sort we have already noted as existing between Sophilos and Kleitias, also existed between Kleitias and Nearchos. The subject concerned is the war between the cranes and the Pygmies. Yet one could scarcely imagine a greater difference in shape than that between the two vases on which the two painters have treated this same theme. The older vase is the big representative krater by Kleitias, where the subject occurs on the frieze adorning the gently sloping foot of the vessel. The other is a little oil-flask only three inches high altogether, an PLATE P. 114 aryballos, where it is painted on the mouth, in a strip that allows the figures a height of only a centimetre. The painter has given his imagination full play in this miniature format. The individual figures are drawn much more superficially, indeed more roughly, than those of Kleitias. But with what agility and impetuosity the fighting is depicted! In the group on the right a crane employs the technique appropriate to these birds by trying to put out the dwarf's eye with the help of its long beak. To the left of this, one of the Pygmies could no longer ward off one of his assailants if a comrade were not hurrying to his aid with club raised ready to strike. The

Oil vessel with the signature of Nearchos. About 550 B.C. *Height 3 in. New York, Metropolitan Museum.*
Cf. pp. 113 ff., 147.

duel on the far left is still undecided; to the right of this group one of the Pygmies is carrying a fallen crane from the battlefield. There are more figures—for example, Perseus with his hat and winged shoes—on the handle. In all these pictures good use is made of a purple colour. But the most successful part of the ornamentation from a ceramic point of view is the series of alternating black and red crescents which, in three horizontal sections, repeat the shape of the vase, so to speak, in paint. Originally the colour effect was still brighter, for every other clay-coloured crescent was painted white; this not very lasting colour has disappeared for the most part today, leaving only a few traces behind. In spite of the sketchy nature of the drawing in the frieze, the little vase is a masterpiece of the Attic miniature style. How this style differs from the hundred year older Corinthian style becomes apparent if we compare the vase with the little perfume flasks in the shape of a woman's head PLATE P. 46 and a self-satisfied duck. The spherical Attic aryballos has at least PLATE P. 83 the charm of brighter colours in its favour.

In spite of this outstanding achievement in the realm of the 'Little Masters', this same Nearchos is in fact one of those Attic painters *Painters and* *potters* who slowly prepare the way for a large-scale style, not only in the absolute size of their figures but also, and chiefly, in the tone of their pictures. While his two sons, Tleson and Ergoteles, likewise successful members of the potters' quarter at Athens, produced—and signed as potters—a number of well-made cups in the 'Little Master' style, their father, in company with other, possibly still more talented vase-painters of these years, painted bigger vases— kantharoi and amphorae—and also pictorial clay plaques (pinakes), which created the atmosphere in which the art of the most important Attic black-figure painter, Exekias, could develop. One of these PLATE P. 154 painters was Lydos. Although the simple forms of the Gorgoneion on a dish painted by him show clearly that there is no longer any room in this style for anything small or miniature, the break-through to a new thematically dramatic style could only occur in the 'action picture'. Now action painting was not in itself anything new in Archaic art at that time; on the contrary, since the end of the seventh century vase-painters had related legends and stories, first on the necks of big amphorae, then in the sixth century on the bodies of black-varnished amphorae, on which a clay 'window' for paintings is reserved. They had related these stories—usually drawn from epic poetry—with a basic, direct joy in events as such and with the primitive desire to depict events as graphically as possible. The sculptors of reliefs approached their themes with the same delight in telling a story. We have seen how on pediments this tendency to present an event in visual terms starts from the corners, which are less important, and gains more and more ground. In the last analysis, what else is the exuberant multitude of pictures on the krater by Kleitias than a manifestation of this pleasure in telling a story?

Spatiality and the shaping of space

The problem of space has already cropped up in connection with Attic sculpture. It is significant that the placing of figures in echelon, overlapping, which at least implies a difference in spatial position between a front and a back layer, and also the three-quarter face, all occur first in pedimental reliefs. The area of the pediment, framed by the geisa, does in itself constitute a space in which the pedimental figures have to be inserted and to which they are forced to adopt, as plastic forms, a certain three-dimensional relationship. But the pediment is only a relatively small part of the temple. The temple as a whole, like any other building, poses the problem of shaping space artistically, an aim that is always present as an immanent possibility wherever anything at all is built. Naturally it can also be neglected without any damage to the structural strength or the religious function of a building. We have seen, for example, that in the interior of the oldest temple of Hera on Samos, where it was even assumed that the enclosure of magic powers was involved, the articulation of space, as an artistic problem, scarcely played any part. The need for an artistic arrangement of the separate spaces and an ordered relationship between the various proportions gradually makes itself noticeable as the interior grows bigger, a change which occurs in its simplest form when the central supports are omitted. This change converts a two-aisled interior into a new unified and bigger space. The greater span of the roof makes it necessary to strengthen the walls here and there—so that

FIG. 5

they can bear the weight of the bigger beams—with pilasters or buttresses; these vertical divisions give a rhythmical articulation to the wall and, through the niches thus created, to the whole interior. This stage of development is represented by the oldest of the temples of Hera at Olympia, which dates from about the middle of the seventh century. This building is by no means a balanced, perfected Archaic temple of the Doric order, but it cannot be denied that it already contains many elements that point forward to the later, perfected design. The characteristic mark of the later, standard type of temple—so far as the interior is concerned—is the two lines of columns which divide the cella into a broad centre aisle and two narrow side aisles. This standard division of the inner chamber of the temple probably came into being spontaneously. However, since there certainly existed examples of Greek architecture in which the wall area was rhythmically articulated in the vertical plane by buttresses, it is permissible to attempt in retrospect the typological derivation of the normal three-aisled plan from these interiors articulated by niches. All we have to do is to remove those sections of the buttresses by which the engaged pillars or half-columns are connected with the longitudinal wall of the temple, and immediately we are left with two lines of columns in the cella. In some cases, including that of the temple of Hera at Olympia, FIG. 24 the niches formed by the buttresses were big enough to invite, so to speak, free-standing columns to occupy the spaces between the parallel buttresses; such designs are in fact the typological link between the interior articulated by buttresses and the three-aisled interior.

In the temple of Hera at Olympia the replacement of the wooden *Temple of Hera at* column by the stone column can still be traced in a rather remark- *Olympia* able way even today. The stylistic details of the individual columns in the peristyle or colonnade round the cella vary considerably; squat shafts alternate with others that are less squat, steep capitals with broader and fatter ones. All this suggests that wooden columns were replaced at very different times by the stone columns still largely preserved today. This deduction is confirmed by a remark in Pausanias' guide-book to the effect that the temple of Hera originally did in fact have wooden columns, one of which was still extant in Pausanias' time, in the *opisthodomos* of the temple, almost as a sort of curiosity for visitors to the Olympian sanctuary. The earliest of the columns still preserved today date from the beginning of the sixth century B.C., which indicates that by then all over Greece stone had become the normal material for all sacral architecture. This is true of both Doric and Ionic buildings.

Temple of Artemis at Ephesos

FIG. 25

Of all the great Ionic buildings erected in the mature Archaic period the best known is the temple of Artemis at Ephesos. It is not the oldest of these giant Ionic temples. It was preceded by the successor to the second, hundred-foot long temple of Hera in Samos, namely the third Samian temple of Hera, built on a vastly bigger scale in the second quarter of the sixth century. There is a link between the two buildings in that Theodoros, one of the architects of the third Heraion, was called over from Samos to Ephesos and assisted in the construction of the temple of Artemis. Assumptions which produced the Samian Heraion and experience gained in building it were of benefit to the new building in Ephesos. The architectural ornaments, and especially the reliefs, are considerably richer on the later temple, which was built in the middle of the sixth century. According to Herodotus (I, 92), Kroisos of Lydia, probably the most hellenized Near Eastern prince of his time, presented this temple with valuable columns, the bottom drums of which were adorned with figures in relief. The excavations at Ephesos have brought to light not only reliefs of this sort but also fragments of dedicatory inscriptions belonging to them, in which King Kroisos is named as donor. Other architectural members, in particular powerful yet simple Ionic capitals, have also been found on the spot. The ground-plan is relatively well known to us. The temple must have had 126 or 128 columns. It was a so-called dipteral temple, that is, there was a double colonnade round the cella, the cella itself had three aisles and there were rows of columns in the opisthodomos. The large number of sharp-edged flutes—40

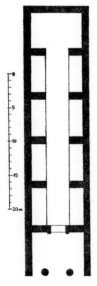

FIG. 24 – *Olympia, Heraion I. About 650 B.C. (Jahrb. des Inst., 61/62, 1946/7, p. 48).*

to 48 on each column—made the columns look slender. Only those in the façade and in front of the entrance hall of the temple were adorned with the figures in relief mentioned above. Thus from outside the temple must have looked at first sight like a forest of columns, if a carefully arranged one; but as one drew nearer one could admire all the details of its rich and delicate workmanship. It was a huge building, but one in which even the mouldings were executed with loving care.

Such mouldings now crop up in Ionic architecture again and again in the most varied situations. The simplest types are the 'dog tooth' and the 'Ionic kymation'. In the Artemision at Ephesos both ornaments occur as upper boundary of the architrave and as a transition to the roof. The Ionic kymation and 'bead and reel' also occur as ornaments crowning the base of the altar of Poseidon on FIG. 26 Cape Monodendri near Didyma in Asia Minor. Another particularly impressive ornamental form that appears there is the volute, which is the leading form in Ionic decorative art as a whole, and in architecture is the chief element in the capital. At the corners of this altar the volutes meet at right angles and curl up high against each other, with plastically modelled palmettes filling the angles. Fine articulation of the sort represented by these examples of *Temple of Apollo* Ionic forms is not a part of contemporary Doric architecture. In- *at Corinth* stead, the notion of 'substance', of specific weight, already mentioned above as the chief characteristic of sixth-century Archaic art, acquires particular significance. This was already evident in the powerful, compact columns of the temple of Artemis at Corcyra, on whose pediments the primitive and terrifying representations of the Gorgon were carved; and it appears again now, some forty years later, towards the middle of the century and contempora- neously with the Artemision of Ephesos, in the temple of Apollo at PLATE P. 123 Corinth. The seven columns still standing, which support one corner of the architrave, are today among the most imposing ruins to be found in Greece. One of the factors contributing to this impression is the use of monolithic columns, that is, columns that each consist of one single piece of stone. The height of each column is four and one-third times their diameter at the bottom. Yet in

spite of these very broad proportions the building does not look shapeless or too massive, and that is because the whole structure is already controlled by a uniform rhythmical impulse otherwise not usually in evidence in architecture before the fifth century. The elements in this rhythmical impulse are the 'entasis', the perceptible but by no means exaggerated convex curve of the columns; the slight inward slope of the corner column, which unites the colonnade with the cella and welds the two into one plastic whole; and finally, a special shaping of the foundations and the stylobate, the 'curvature', otherwise found only in Greek Classical architecture, and here, in this Corinthian temple of Apollo, carried through only at the ends. By 'curvature' we mean the deliberate, regular and precisely calculated downward slope, at the corners and towards the corners, of the horizontal platform (stylobate) which carries the columns, so that when one looks along the edge of the step, this turns out to be not a straight line but a regular curve. This shaping, too, serves the same end, the rhythmical unification of the building; but while the entasis and the very slight inward slope of the columns are immediately perceptible to the attentive beholder, the unifying, indeed decisive, effect of the curvature is produced without our being aware of it; it is not directly visible.

The unified and at the same time articulated structure is paralleled by a simple ground-plan which is much shortened in comparison with the elongated proportions of the early period. In big Ionic temples like the Artemision of Ephesos the original proportions of 1:5 had already been replaced by a scheme which made the sides about twice as long as the ends. It is the same with the temple at Corinth. In the Doric temple, too, the fundamental difference in the proportions strikes us at once if we compare the temple of Hera at Olympia and the temple of Apollo at Thermon on the one hand with the temple of Apollo at Corinth on the other. Only the number of columns—the proportion is 6:15—still echoes to some extent the traditional concept of a decidedly elongated temple.

FIG. 25 – *Ephesos, Archaic Artemision. Middle of 6th century B.C. (Krischen, Die griechische Stadt, Plate 33).*

FIG. 26 – *Altar on Cape Monodendri near Miletos. Second quarter of 6th century B.C. (H. Berve–G. Gruben, Griechische Tempel und Heiligtümer, p. 234, Fig. 111).*

Architecture and architectural reliefs in Magna Graecia

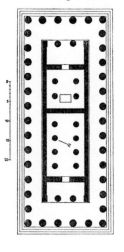

The Doric architecture of the Greek colonies in southern Italy lags a little way behind in the shaping and development of structural forms; the same is true of statuary and relief sculpture in these Greek colonial territories. We shall return to this phenomenon in architecture when we come to discuss the temple of Athena at Paestum. So far as sculpture is concerned, it is as well to recall at this point that metope reliefs which in Athens, Delphi or Corinth would be dated to the beginning of the sixth century, or even as immediately subsequent to architectural reliefs like the goddess with the veil from Mycenae, must be put substantially later in Magna Graecia. In such cases the principle in the history of art that one must always date according to the stylistically latest

FIG. 27 – *Corinth, temple of Apollo. About 550 B.C. (H. Berve–G. Gruben, Griechische Tempel und Heiligtümer, p. 143, Fig. 39).*

Temple of Apollo at Corinth. *Cf. p. 119.*

individual form is unconditionally valid. Thus for example a series of metopes—the oldest one preserved at Selinus—is by no means so old, judged by the standard of absolute chronology, as it was once generally believed to be. The relief showing Europa on the FIG. 28 bull—one of this series of metopes—is certainly reminiscent of heraldic compositions of the early period such as the painted metopes of the temple at Thermon, and this impression is strength- PLATE P. 78 ened by the strict stylization of the relief as a whole and the shallow frontal view of the bull's head, which is turned at right angles out of the plane of the relief. But one soon notices the exceptionally successful characterization of the swimming motion of the bull's

FIG. 28 – *Metope showing Europa. Limestone. From Selinus. About 550 B.C. Palermo, Museo Nazionale.*

front hooves. The dolphin at the lower edge of the picture symbolizes the sea over which the bull is carrying Europa. However, what makes it certain that this relief—at first sight so old-fashioned— must be ascribed to the middle of the sixth century is the clear and relatively free rendering of the chiton between the lower thighs of the woman being abducted by the bull; she sits nervously on its back, supporting herself and gripping the right horn so as not to slip off into the water. In the same way, the long series of metopes from the sanctuary of Hera at Foce del Sele near Paestum, many of which show an amazing delicacy and vivacity in their stylized details, is not a product of the period under discussion, in spite of the often almost primitive style of the composition as a whole; it dates from well on in the second half of the sixth century.

Types of capital   Let us now try once again to grasp the architectural forms at the point where they speak to us most unambiguously, in the capitals, which also illuminate most clearly the character of the Doric and FIG. 29   Ionic orders. The prototype of the finished Doric capital is preserved —in an early stage of its development, it is true—in the gravestone of a man called Xenvares on the island of Corcyra. The top slab of the capital, the abacus, bears this inscription: 'Memorial am I

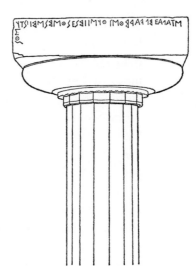

FIG. 29 – *Doric capital of a grave column. Limestone. First quarter of 6th century B.C. Corcyra Museum (G. Rodenwaldt, Altdorische Bildwerke in Korfu, Plate 1).*

on the grave mound of Xenvares, the son of Meixis'. The technical function of a horizontal slab between column and entablature was to protect the open end of a perpendicular beam from the effect of the weather, especially damp, and of course it is only in wooden buildings that this function provides a meaningful explanation of architectural forms. On the other hand, it is quite possible that in one phase of the transition from wooden to stone architecture the columns still consisted of wood while the horizontal slabs, the capitals, were already made of stone. In any case, this kind of technical explanation of the shape of the capital would fit only one section of the Doric capital, the abacus, and likewise only the volute section of the Ionic capital. An illuminating explanation of the echinus, the pillow under the abacus, has been suggested by G. Rodenwaldt: he assumes that, in the original wooden architecture, at the spot where the horizontal slab, or cross-block (the later abacus), covered the perpendicular beam or column, the upper end of this beam was wrapped in rope and binding soaked in resin to give it better protection against the weather. The echinus is the formal link between the angular, square-shaped abacus and the round column. Whereas the broad-pressed, widely projecting shape

125

of the oldest examples seem to suggest the downward pressure of the heavy entablature and roof, the later forms of the Doric echinus fulfil the laws of statics in a different way. They provide a harmonious link between the support and its load by means of the visible tension of the convex curve between the top of the circular column and the square abacus.

The Doric capital is the most palpable embodiment of what we mean by the 'increase in substance' in the Greek architecture of this period. The Ionic capital, which came into being in its standard form at the same time, reflects the same process of transition from wooden to stone architecture, though in a somewhat less obvious FIG. 30 way. Its specialized variant, the so-called Aeolic capital, does not represent the original form of the Ionic type of capital; it developed as an ornament in miniature art, articles of daily use and vase decoration, passed from there into furniture-making and eventually into constructional carpentry. In architecture it only played a part for a fairly short space of time and within a narrow geographical area. The situation is quite different with the standard Ionic capital. Right from its origin round about 600 B.C., all through antiquity and in every part of the ancient world, it is an excellent gauge for measuring stylistic changes in architectural ornamentation. The reason for this is that its more complicated forms react more sensitively to historical development than those of the simpler Doric capital. Volutes, which are the predominating element in both the Aeolic and the Ionic capital, are characteristic of Ionian ornamentation as a whole. It is quite possible that there were already big volutes on the capitals of the second temple of Hera in Samos; if there were, they were carved out of wood. The oldest stone Ionic capitals that have been preserved belonged to votive offerings in the sanctuaries of Apollo on Delos and at Delphi; they are made of Naxian marble. Like the oldest Doric capitals, they are very broad; the middle part of the volute-member is low; the vertically divided cushion underneath shows the so-called egg-and-tongue moulding, i.e., a hanging tongue or leaf ornament. This kind of ornament remained as characteristic of Ionic architecture as the big coils of the volutes, and architectural profiles adorned with these down-

FIG. 30 – *Aeolic capital from Klopedi on Lesbos. Limestone. Middle of 6th century B.C. Mytilene Museum. (Annuario della Scuola Arch. di Atene, 1946/48, p. 31, Fig. 4).*

ward pointing leaves are therefore known as Ionic kymatia. The connection of opposing volutes by a palmette growing up perpendicularly from the point of contact is a motif constantly repeated by the antefixes at the edge of the roof of big temples. The same syntax of ornament leads to richer formations in the shape of the decorations known as akroteria which are placed on the roofs of temples, over the middle of the gable. There the volute motif is usually built up in several stages over the apex of the roof, and palmettes are also inserted at the points where the volute begins to spiral inwards. Very similar compositions occur as the crowning points of slender

FIG. 31 – *Grave stele. Marble. After 550 B.C. Boston, Museum of Fine Arts (Jahrb. d. Inst., 79, 1964, p. 190, Fig. 48).*

127

Ionic capital. Middle of 6th century B.C. *Width 2 ft. 7 in. Samos, Heraion. Cf. p. 129.*

grave stelai. The stele itself does not need to bear a relief. In some cases the picture intended to recall the dead man was not carved but simply painted; in other cases the perpendicular oblong of the stele bears only an inscription, usually a short one. On the front of a grave stele in the Fine Arts Museum at Boston, topped by a shallow moulding and framed by slender rods, only faint traces of paint can still be discerned, but the stele itself, which comes from northern

Asia Minor, is one of the best-preserved examples of an ornamental top of the sort described. To judge by the style and in particular by the regularity of the lotus bud and the palmettes, which show little trace of the incipient loosening up of forms, this stone dates from the forties of the sixth century. In a capital from Samos which must PLATE P. 128 belong to one of the smaller temples in the sanctuary of Hera— although it could not be assigned with certainty to one of those buildings whose ground-plans are known—the originally broad, shallow forms of the older Ionic capitals are substantially modified. There is no question here of shallow planes; the capital has become an eminently plastic shape. It is true that the volutes are still very much part of the capital block; but the coils of the spirals and the horizontal tie between them show tension and powerful elasticity. The leaf ornament juts out with positive exuberance from under-neath the volute section. Forms like these in architecture give full play to the substance of the material and yet are controlled to the last detail by the plastic modelling. Such forms are only possible for one short moment of time. They stand at the point where the pendulum of historical development halts for a moment before swinging back. This Samian capital displays the complacent beauty of the mature Archaic period. Henceforth bodies and limbs— including the plastic elements of architecture—become freer; they may also appear more spiritualized, and correspondingly they are lighter, less weighty.

IV. RIPE ARCHAIC: LATE PERIOD

(*circa* 550–490 B.C.)

Art in the time of
Peisistratos

SCULPTURE

PLATE P. 131

APPX. PL. 4

The style of Athenian art in the fifty years from Peisistratos' first *coup d'état* to the expulsion of his son Hippias remains remarkably constant, even though the political history of this period is by no means without incident: it includes the expulsion and return of Peisistratos, his death and succession by his sons, the expulsion of the Alkmeonidai, a rich noble family, and finally the murder of Hipparchos, one of the two brother-tyrants. Yet when one compares one of the slightly larger-than-life Attic kouros statues of the third quarter of the sixth century with the kouros in New York, which is some three generations older, one would at first be inclined to think that during this none too short period of time nothing had altered. But let us look a little more closely at the statue from Anavyssos in the Athenian National Museum. It becomes increasingly clear that the powerful influence of the kouros type, once this kind of statue had been created, dominated sculptors for decades. Nevertheless, although the prescribed pattern remains the same, the proportions have altered. Above all, the head has become smaller in proportion to the body. In addition, both body and limbs have acquired the capacity for organic movement; even at rest they are tensed. It follows from this that the anatomy is more organically modelled. The muscles bulge out more. But the biggest difference lies in the differentiation of the physiognomy. It may be an accident that the stepped base of the later figure has also come down to us, with an inscription saying that the name of the person represented was 'Kroisos', but at any rate the figure is no longer anonymous, as the figure by the Dipylon Master is. All these subtle but not inconsiderable differences are repeated in every single detail, especially the modelling of the mouth and eyes, and in the more delicate and more complex styling of the hair.

The name 'Kroisos' (Croesus) given by the inscription is curious. There can hardly be any doubt that for some reason or other an

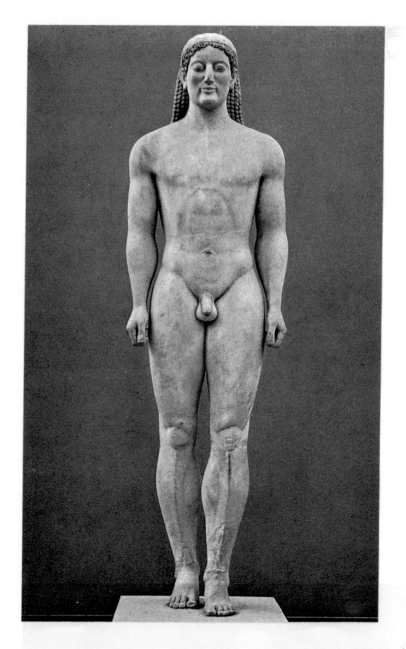

Funerary statue of Kroisos. Marble. From Anavyssos in Attica. Third quarter of 6th century B.C. *Height 6 ft. 5 in. Athens, National Museum. Cf. pp. 130 ff.*

Attic father named his son, born shortly before the middle of the century, after the hellenized king of Lydia. After all, many of the qualities enumerated above, which characterize this Attic statue of the second half of the century and differentiate it from a seventh-century one, are also derived from the East.

APPX. PL. 5 It has long been dubious whether a sitting statue found in the old capital of Samos, unfortunately lacking a head and, according to an inscription on the side of the throne dedicated by one Aeakes to the goddess Hera, represents this Aeakes or the goddess herself. Probability favours Aeakes, who could well have had himself shown in the attitude of oriental rulers—and also of the Greek priest-kings of Didyma in Asia Minor, in proximity to the East; neither the hair-style, with the six locks falling on the shoulders, nor the full breast are decisive arguments against this interpretation in the case of a wealthy and influential man. The date of this statue is much disputed. Sound reasons have been adduced for assigning it both to the forties and to the twenties of the sixth century, or indeed even to the beginning of the fifth century. This is partly because two Samians called Aeakes are known to us as historical personalities. One was the father and the other a nephew of the Samian tyrant Polykrates. The net result of this scholarly controversy is that the earlier date can certainly be defended and is therefore theoretically possible. In fact, the statue is best understood as belonging either to the years immediately before Polykrates—son of an already important family—brought off his successful *coup d'état*, or else to the early years of his tyranny. That an otherwise completely unknown Aeakes, who had nothing to do with the family of Polykrates, dedicated the statue—another possibility that has been considered—is extremely unlikely because of the good quality and considerable cost of the figure. For in any case it represents an advance on the traditional formal structure of Ionian art, though it is true that this advance goes hand in hand with the emphatic retention of a type of statue developed in the East. This observation is not self-contradictory; rather does it support the connection of the statue with the particular historical and geographical situation, and with the particular historical character represented here.

When we compare the statue of Aeakes with the standing statue of PLATE P. 96
Ornithe, which is also Samian, the stylistic difference which must
have arisen in a bare twenty years seems at first to be almost greater
than the one we have observed between the kouros in New York
and the statue of Kroisos. In place of a surface uniformly covered
with folds, as in the statue of Ornithe, we now find a surface that
is strongly modelled and endowed with life-like movement: the
legs are clearly outlined through the robe, bundles of folds are
pushed together, and the tresses of hair are not unified and compact,
as in the case of Ornithe, but parted from one another. On the other
hand, the vertical tendency in the lines of the composition is
retained. Remarkably enough, however, in spite of these signs of a
loosening up, the seated statue of Aeakes is by no means a very
'naturalistically' conceived piece of sculpture, for the individual
elements in it, though freed more and more from the statuary block
and from the uniform plane, are subjected, each one of them, to a
much more absolute stylization. Such boldness in the modelling is
evidence of a more individual artistic temperament, just as the
wilfulness of the formal idiom can also be interpreted as a reflection
of Aeakes' own wishes. In Attica or the Peloponnese a member of an
old established noble family would not have let himself be portrayed
in such expressive stylistic forms; and nowhere in Attica until well
into the fifth century did artists employ such unconventional means
of expression. Yet works such as this provoked all over Greece a
change that makes itself apparent in a psychologically more
delicately shaded, more individual characterization, especially of
the face. This could already be observed in the Kroisos from Anavyssos and it is also apparent in contemporary grave reliefs. Signifi- RELIEFS
cantly, it is in Attica that we now meet the above-mentioned exceptions from the general rule that Archaic grave reliefs are confined
to slender, upright stelai and in general portray only male figures.
The most important of these exceptions—most important because it
was to have the most influence on the future—is a marble fragment PLATE P. 134
discovered only a few years ago, which is among the most interesting
and also most appealing items in the museum at Athens.
This relief, too, was originally taller than it was broad, but it should

Mother and child. Fragment of a grave relief. Marble. About 540 B.C. *Height 15 in. Athens, National Museum. Cf. p. 133.*

certainly not be visualized as once having been as narrow and tall as the stelai showing youthful athletes. It depicts a mother and child; their heads are preserved on the fragment. The mother's face is inclined very slightly forward and her glance rests on the face of her little son, whose head she supports with her left hand. Obviously she was shown in a sitting position and held the little boy on her lap. Her cloak envelops both figures: it appears in paint on the background of the relief between mother and son, with the crenellated ornamentation of the edge, once brightly coloured, rounding off the picture at the top, and it appears again, in relief this time, running obliquely across the back of the hand. Thus the group is bound together outwardly by the piece of clothing and inwardly by the bond of love and kinship. Something of this is visible in the careful gesture with which the slender fingers and the palm of the hand tenderly lift the child's head, which itself is without any power of movement. The eyelid—originally picked out in paint—is closed, the eye can no longer return the mother's glance. As for the smile that plays round the lips—does it reflect the idea of being drawn into a happier dream world or only the feeling of spiritual happiness that is peculiar to so many, if not quite all, of the creations of this particular phase of Archaic art?

The question also arises whether details of the style of the relief can tell us from which part of the Greek world this curious composition of two figures, which stands quite alone in contemporary Athens, was introduced. We are not in a position to answer this question. Although the child's profile is reminiscent of one or two heads on Ionian black-figure vases, which are very rare, it may well be the work of an Attic sculptor. The shape of the ear and the technical treatment of the hair, which is roughed up to take colour, are also paralleled in Attic art. So we can safely assume that this relief is native work, especially after comparing it with the figures on the bases of Attic reliefs, although these figures, admittedly, are much smaller. The relief would then introduce, as an isolated forerunner, the long series of Attic grave reliefs depicting family scenes which from about 420 to 310 B.C. were the usual memorials on Athenian graves. One of these later reliefs, that of Ampharete, comes very close to this fragment in content. It is the monument on the grave of an elderly woman and her grandchild. An inscription describes the significance of the relief: 'Ampharete. I hold here the dear child of my daughter. I held it on my knees like this when we both beheld the rays of the sun with our eyes in life, and now, dead, I hold the dead child.' One wonders whether the Archaic relief also had an inscription over it once, providing information about the relationship of the two figures, their fate and their death. For more extensive epitaphs now begin to occur in Attica, less laconic in tone than the column on the grave of Xenvares. Take for example

FIG. 32 the epitaph of Phrasikleia:

> Tomb of Phrasikleia.
> Maiden shall I be called
> For ever; instead of marriage
> From the gods this
> Name I won.

Forms of writing These epitaphs are excellent evidence for the history and art history of their time, not only in their content but also in the forms of writing employed. We can trace a development which leads from

FIG. 29 the heavy, old-fashioned letters of the Xenvares inscription—closely related to Corinthian letters—via the somewhat carelessly written

FIG. 32 Phrasikleia inscription, which betrays a certain lack of self-assurance

FIG. 36 —to an inscribed base which a Samian sculptor carved in Samian letters for a Samian who died at Athens in the last decade but one of the sixth century.

Inscription and ornament If one concentrates one's attention on the 'handwriting', the flow of the writing, instead of the content, letters can be seen as a form of ornament. That is also how they were mainly employed by the vase-painters of this period. A point is finally reached where some vase-painters insert meaningless rows of letters between the figures in their pictures as a sort of filling ornament which at that time was 'modern'. At the same time this phenomenon also shows that a greater number of motifs were available for ornamental purposes than there had been earlier. The clearest contrast to this is the narrow range of motifs used in *Geometric* ornamentation, with its limited varieties of meander, concentric circle, triangle, lozenge

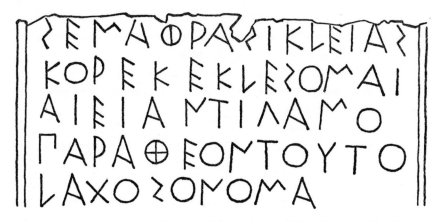

FIG. 32 – *Inscription from the pillar-capital for the grave of Phrasikleia. Marble. From Attica. About 540 B.C. Merenda (Panagia). (L. H. Jeffery, The Local Scripts of Archaic Greece, Plate 3, no. 29.)*

and zigzag band. Certainly even now the traditional motifs of volute, palmette, lotus band and leaf-and-dart remain the main reservoir on which artists draw. But there are also freer forms, mainly based on the vegetable kingdom—blossoms and tendrils. But above all there is a tendency in all branches of art to adopt a more ornamental treatment. This is probably the consequence of a slowly appearing lack of inner greatness in figure pictures and all artistic creations in general. They incline towards the 'fairy-tale world' of the late Archaic epoch. New realms are opened up, but the price of the advance is a loss in 'weight'. In return, the decorative value of works of art, especially miniatures, increases.

In these circumstances it can be no surprise that from about 540 B.C. to the end of the Archaic period miniature art provides the main centre of interest for us. Objects of daily use, implements of every sort, bronze and clay statuettes, vessels shaped like figures and others made of clay and metal are just as important for the history of art in this period as temples and statues. They now have at their service a perfection of technique acquired over the years by generations of craftsmen. In addition, further technical possibilities are discovered and experiments made in their application. Yet it

MINIATURE ART

is also characteristic of this late phase of Archaic perfection that technical virtuosity or even technical experimentation never governs style; even now these are only controlled means to an end.

Bronze-casting Bronze-casting develops at a positively furious pace. The workshops in the Peloponnese continued to be the most productive ones, but it was a fruitful period at Athens as well. In Samos the new technical process of hollow-casting was developed and experiments were made with various kinds of metal alloys. There were also workshops in Boeotia, Aegina and Naxos and probably other places as well. The products of the colonial cities in southern Italy and Sicily are outstanding in artistic quality. Obviously Corinthian bronze-casters founded workshops in Syracuse and Spartan craftsmen one in Tarentum, while bronze-casters from the islands went to the Ionian colonies and settled down there.

It is no longer possible today to estimate just how extensively metal vessels were used. For daily use they were far superior to clay vessels because they were less fragile. It is true that they cost more than unpainted clay ware, but on the other hand ceramic ware with painted decorations was probably much more expensive than plain metal vessels. But metal vessels that were artistically engraved and decorated with ornaments, or which had cast appliqués, figured handles and an ornamental foot or base, were at least as costly as high-quality painted vessels of clay. Whereas the clay vessels have at any rate left behind a large number of sherds, which could not be used a second time, metal was repeatedly melted down again during long periods of civilization, so that the original number of metal vessels has been reduced by a far greater proportion. As for the metal pots, pans, jugs and dishes that at some time or other became hidden in the ground, almost always the thin, beaten vessels themselves have oxidized so badly in the damp earth that the sides of vessels as such have completely disappeared and only the heavy, cast parts—handle, mouth, circular base, soldered-on reliefs—have been preserved. Besides such structural components of the vessels there were sometimes further additions which—especially in valuable votive offerings—were intended to increase the value of the gift still more. Thus as early as the eighth and seventh centuries

Centaur. Bronze. About 540 B.C. *Height 14 in. New York, Metropolitan Museum. Cf. pp. 140 ff.*

there were statuettes supporting the handles of the big vessels to which they were riveted; bronze figures serving as lid handles; and bridges fixed across part of the mouth of a vessel with one or more PLATE P. 139 figures soldered on to them. The Centaur in the Metropolitan Museum in New York may come from the edge of a large bowl. It is also conceivable that it was originally on a piece of furniture—a throne or a couch—or that it adorned a box plated with bronze. Its function can thus not be decided for certain. But what is almost certain is that it was used in some kind of tectonic context, on a vessel or implement; it is very improbable that this figure was originally intended to be an independent votive offering, and quite out of the question that the statuette could have stood on its own as an ornament in a private house; there is no evidence for ornaments of this kind until the fourth century. On the contrary, it can be assumed that the statuette is not autonomous in another sense too, in that a centaur armed with a torn-off branch and rushing in to the attack at the gallop must have had an adversary. He was therefore probably part of a group consisting of at least two figures. Such a group could well be explained as a sort of excerpt from the 'Thessalian battle with the Centaurs', a theme rich in characters which was much favoured on Attic vases and Cycladic bronze reliefs at this time. It would then be a natural step to see in our statuette an adversary of Kaineus, an invulnerable hero who could only be put out of action by being rammed into the ground alive by the strong blows of two Centaurs. The determined force with which this Centaur is swinging his weapon would fit in very well with the theme of this particular group. The date suggested for the statuette is about 540 B.C. The face and breast retain much of the older firmness of shaping; what is new about this little work is the successful plastic modelling of the boldly moving horse's body. The workmanship is almost certainly Peloponnesian, possibly Argive.

PLATE P. 142 Somewhat later than the Centaur is a pair of bronze handles, each consisting of a ring and a water bird which holds the ring with its bent back head. The bodies of the birds—the necks seem too long for a duck, yet almost too short for a swan—were each fastened by three rivets to the gently curving side of a bulging vessel, probably a cauldron. When one compares these creatures with the compact form of the clay duck in the Berlin Museum, one feels inclined to speak rather of swans in connection with the bronze handles and thus to do justice to the graceful freedom apparent in every single detail of the shaping of the heads and feathers. The vessel to which the handles belonged, and thus the handles too, could well be Attic.

From about the same time or again a little later dates a big bronze PLATE P. 144 vase that was among the finds in the most amazing tomb opened in recent years. This was the grave of a Celtic princess which was discovered in north-eastern France, near Vix. The contents of the grave are now in the museum at Châtillon-sur-Seine. Besides a complete chariot of native Celtic workmanship which had been placed in the grave in a dismantled state, there were also articles imported from the Greek world. A clay drinking-cup decorated with a black-figure picture of a battle and some simple metal cups are of hardly more than average quality, but another cup made of silver, with gold plate over the centre of the inside, provides a foretaste of the more valuable grave furniture. Brooches worn on the clothing, bracelets and rings were among the dead woman's jewellery. One unique article is a heavy gold diadem which was found around the skull when the grave was opened. It terminates on each side in a plastically modelled animal's foot, and these in turn rest on pear-shaped thickenings. Attached to these are two bases made of filigree work, each of which supports the statuette of a winged horse—all of 24-carat gold. But still more amazing is the huge bronze vase with two handles curling round in volutes at the top—a so-called volute krater—and a lid usable as a sieve. The weight of the metal in this krater amounts to nearly 618 pounds and its capacity is no less than 262 gallons. Bronze vessels as big as this were unknown to us before the discovery of the grave at Vix, whose contents, thanks to favourable conditions, have been preserved so well. This particular kind of vessel was known in antiquity as a 'Lakonian krater' (krater Lakonikos). The numerous ornaments, the relief appliqués on the neck and handles of the vessel,

Cauldron handles in the shape of swans. Bronze. 540–530 B.C. *Height without rings 2³/₅ in. Cambridge, Fitzwilliam Museum. Cf. pp. 140 f.*

are also in the Lakonian style—in a somewhat softer variant of it, to be precise, which has been recognized as the style of a branch workshop in Tarentum, in Magna Graecia. Let us look more closely PLATE P. 144 at one of the reliefs applied to the neck, a four-horse team. In spite of the exaggerated size of the krater the relief work shows no signs of coarseness or hardness. The appliqué has been cast in a mould and then worked over everywhere with the chisel so thoroughly that the 'skin' formed by the mould has completely disappeared. Hence the technical perfection, the charm and immediacy of the impression, which is not disturbed at any point by traces of the mode of manufacture.

The eight teams of four horses, with helmeted charioteers, which encircle the neck of the krater like a frieze, are not to be conceived as setting out for battle, although a heavily-armed warrior stands behind each of the teams. This procession is too reminiscent of the funeral cortèges on Geometric vases for us to think here at first of anything but the retinue of an important funeral. This implies the assumption that the whole vessel was made in the first place with a view to a funerary purpose.

The quality of the relief on the bronze krater of Vix is such that in this respect even a very well-made bronze statuette in Boston lags a little way behind it. The attribution of the statuette to a bronze-casting workshop in Sicyon is probably correct; in its plastic structure this bronze is certainly more closely related to the Centaur in New York than to the four-horse teams of Vix. The subject is Hermes, shown as the god of flocks and herds, carrying a little ram. PLATE P. 146 The god is characterized by his hat and above all by his winged shoes; originally the right hand obviously also held Hermes' staff, the kerykeion. In its division and modelling the face is more reminiscent of that of the Centaur in New York than of anything else, yet at the same time the difference in date is clearly perceptible; the figure of Hermes is the later of the two. It was in small statues like these, made with minute precision, that the bronze sculptors of the north-eastern Peloponnese did their best work at this time. A decade or two later the best-known master of contemporary Sicyon obtained a representative commission far from his native land: he was asked to cast the cult statue for the temple of Apollo Philesios at Didyma. There are echoes of this statue, which was certainly much over life-size, in later works; but they tell us little more about the original than that it was basically of the kouros type, only enriched to the extent that the left hand held a bow and arrow and the right—curiously enough—a stag. These clues to the appearance of the statue, which are provided by some bronze statuettes and a marble relief of the Roman period, are confirmed by the description given by Pliny in his *Natural History* (34,75) of the Apollo Philesios

Relief from the neck of the krater from Vix. Bronze. About 530 B.C. *Height of the vase 5 ft. 5 in.*
Châtillon-sur-Seine. Cf. pp. 38, 141, 142.

by Kanachos. Naturally all these indications and allusions do not
tell us very much about the style of this cult statue.

LARGE
BRONZES

In these circumstances it is hardly an exaggeration to say that some
years ago a miracle was vouchsafed to us. In 1959, in the Peiraieus,
the port of Athens, during the course of some work on the roads,
several Greek bronze statues were accidentally discovered. They
had probably been laid there at some time in the first century B.C.,

ready for transport by sea to Italy, but had been overlooked in the unfavourable conditions prevailing, gradually buried and completely forgotten until today. Among these statues there is a naked Apollo, somewhat over life-size, which is half a century older than the famous 'Charioteer of Delphi' and therefore the oldest large Greek bronze that we possess so far. And it is an 'original', not a copy made in the Roman period. This statue, too, originally held the bow in its left hand, but in its right it held the cup for pouring a libation. Nevertheless, the motif is similar to that of the Apollo Philesios. The newly-discovered figure is about ten years earlier than Kanachos' masterpiece, but the two works probably came from the same region, the neighbouring cities of Corinth and Sicyon in the north-eastern Peloponnese. We are thus now in a position to form some idea of Kanachos' statue, which was possibly somewhat bigger in size and almost certainly more splendid in appearance. A certain heaviness in the individual forms, and indeed a certain mournfulness in the expression, can be explained—though only partly, of course—by technical considerations. In the first decades of the development of large-scale hollow-casting there must have been fairly close technical links, and hence also to a certain extent formal links, between casting and wood-carving. It had already been possible to observe in the case of the charioteer of Delphi and other fragments of early big bronzes that the model for casting was made out of wood, not clay. Moreover, according to tradition, although Kanachos made the statue of Apollo Philesios from bronze, his other masterpiece, the statue of Apollo Ismenios at Thebes, was carved in cedar wood. And in fact, in the statue from the Peiraieus too, the hard shape of the chin and the jaw, the cut of the eyelids and above all the almost undivided, unchiselled rendering of the locks of hair recall the technique of wood-carving. But the statue is invaluable because it represents the only late Archaic large-scale piece of sculpture from the Peloponnesian region preserved in the original. For the reasons given above large-scale statues are rather rare in the late Archaic period. Nevertheless, so far as Attica is concerned we are fairly well provided thanks to the finds on the Athenian Acropolis. For example, there is the larger-than-life kore

statue dedicated on the Acropolis by the potter Nearchos and made by the sculptor Antenor, and the gigantomachy pediment from the Peisistratid temple of Athena; then there are other temple pediments, such as that of the temple of Apollo at Delphi and the Amazon pediment of the temple of Apollo at Eretria, which shows at least Attic influence; in addition there are funerary monuments, such as the statue of the youth Aristodikos, erected, like the statue of Kroisos, but some thirty years later, on a grave in the neighbourhood of Anavyssos. For the Peloponnese, on the other hand, we have nothing to which to turn but the statue of Apollo from the Peiraieus. It not only provides tangible evidence of the stage preceding the art of the famous Peloponnesian sculptors—such as Kanachos and Hageledas—from the period of transition between the Archaic and the Classical age; it also throws some light on an artistic centre which, with an independently developed, harder, simpler, and heavier style, restricts Ionian influence in Athens and is itself to exert some influence

Hermes carrying a ram. Bronze. 530–520 B.C. *Height 10 in. Boston, Museum of Fine Arts. Cf. p. 143.*

there at the beginning of the fifth century. Finally, this is the germ from which the art of Polykleitos was to grow two or three generations later.

There are abundant remains of vase-painting from the phase of its entire maturity, as there are from the whole Archaic period, with no gaps in the material from the point of view of historical development; but—as we have already emphasized—this is true only of Athenian products. Attic pottery is now dominated by Exekias and Amasis. VASE-PAINTING

Workshop industry as a mode of artistic activity, workshop traditions, the shifting of a vase-painter from one workshop to another, rivalry between one workshop and another—these are the conditions under which the masterpieces of black-figure and red-figure ware were produced during the heyday of these techniques. The same conditions as such no doubt prevailed in the Geometric period as well, but probably in those days division of the work within the same workshop, specialization, separation of the painter from the potter, were not yet usual. The first evidence we have of this kind of division is provided by the signatures of Ergotimos and Kleitias. We have already mentioned that Exekias and also Amasis probably painted pots which they had made themselves.

Let us first try to visualize the situation which Exekias and Amasis found prevailing in this branch of art when they themselves were young. We have already become acquainted with the style of Kleitias, with his somewhat petty and pedantic, but on the other hand also magnificent creations. About the time when Nearchos painted the aryballos with Pygmies and cranes, Kleitias painted and signed a Gorgon's head on a little stand, an object possibly intended to support a delicate drinking-cup. Connoisseurs might well have recognized Kleitias' style in this picture even if it were not signed, for here too that fine stroke of his and that somewhat fiddling, very fine but also somewhat pedantic manner are clearly perceptible. PLATE P. 114

A Gorgoneion painted in the same years but by another hand on a shallow plate is completely different in style. The plate is not signed, but the painter can be named by means of stylistic comparison. He was a younger contemporary of Kleitias—and an older con- PLATE P. 154

Lydos

Detail of a bronze statue of Apollo. About 520 B.C. *Height 6 ft. 4 in. Athens, National Museum. Cf. pp. 145 ff.*

temporary of Exekias—called Lydos. Even in Lydos' picture the demonic wildness of the Gorgon, as depicted on the pediment in Corcyra, has been clearly toned down, in spite of the bared tusks APPX. PL. 18 and the addition of the beard. But the plate shows just as clearly Lydos' ability and deliberate intention to paint in the large-figure style; for the plate could perfectly well have been decorated with the same motif embodied in a different kind of composition. For example, the Gorgon's head, treated as a relatively small central emblem, could have been framed in a frieze, with the latter possibly also divided up into several zones. Plates decorated in this way actually exist: two examples, painted by Sophilos, have come down to us. Kleitias follows, as we have already seen, in Sophilos' footsteps. But Lydos declines to follow in those of Kleitias. So this trail peters out even before the beginning of the century when Lydos, with some of his contemporaries and fellow-guildsmen, founds a different tradition, by which Nearchos for one was not uninfluenced in some of his pictures. One of these contemporaries of Lydos, probably not Lydos himself but an anonymous painter who adorned a cauldron, dedicated on the Acropolis, with chariots and a cavalry battle, may have been Exekias' teacher. But the pupil soon far surpassed the teacher.

Three things make Exekias unique in the whole history of Greek *Exekias* vase-painting. To start with, he was the first to seize a legendary event, that is, a happening in time, an action, at the best moment for artistic treatment and to put every appropriate detail in its place within a four-sided frame. With that the western kind of picture, as we still know it today, was brought into being. Second, in some of his pictures he gave this pregnant moment a point, a tragic note, in such a way that the continuous narrative undergoes a positively dramatic heightening, with overtones of climax and final crash. And third, again only in some of his pictures, he achieved such a strong inward concentration that the picture is governed not by the outward action but by the psychological event, which is presented in visual terms.

Vase-paintings of the Geometric period relate, so far as we can speak with any certainty about them, to contemporary events. We saw this in the examples of pictures of battles and war, of lyings in state, funeral processions and funeral games. Only in the age of colonization, of more intensive trade and the inrush of oriental motifs into Greek vase decoration, can we point to pictures that are unequivocally mythological. The wish for such pictures may also have been provoked by contact with the Near East. During the course of the seventh century B.C. the number of mythological pictures in Greek miniature art, especially on vases but also in metal engraving and reliefs, continually increases and for a time they completely oust scenes from everyday life. We have seen that, so far as themes are concerned, the great epic cycles of the *Iliad* and the *Odyssey* enjoy a favoured position. We can assume that a fairly large number of other themes, too, had found their final poetic, if not literary, form before they appeared in pictorial art. Finally, many sagas may have been transmitted only by the oral tradition of a limited area. In the case of those vase-painters of whose personalities we can form some notion, whose artistic temperaments we can grasp, even the choice of themes is characteristic. This is true of Sophilos and Kleitias, of Lydos and Nearchos, but above all of Exekias.

On the oldest of the amphoras bearing the signature of Exekias as potter the treatment of the theme is typical as well as the choice of it. One side shows the departure of a warrior, who stands beside the charioteer on a chariot drawn by four horses. The warrior, whose name is given as Anchippos, cannot be fitted into any of the known cycles of legends, but a curious addition by the painter points to a sad outcome for the enterprise on which Anchippos is setting forth. Between him and the horses a bird with a human head, a siren, is drawn, flying over the team of horses. Obviously the demon of death appears here as a bad omen. The other side of the same vase is adorned with a picture of the fight between Herakles and the three-bodied monster Geryon. In the middle, between the two adversaries, lies the dying herdsman Eurytion. Such fine details as the clouding sight of the eye, rendered with the black-figure technique of incision, occur for the first time in Exekias.

Such details give the pictures of Exekias right from the start an atmosphere of tragedy. And it is peculiar to Exekias alone that after his powers have reached their full development he shows a preference for the tragic figure of Ajax as the hero of his pictures. Exekias begins by making the mythological theme obey the rules—discovered by himself—of a strict pictorial composition, in other words by consciously subjecting the content to the artistic conception. But he had already progressed beyond this early stage in his own development when he created the amphora now in the museum PLATE P. 153 at Boulogne. Like Nearchos, Exekias was both potter and painter. The squat, but not too widely bellying body of the vase, with its strong handles and the emphatically conclusive edge to the mouth, corresponds perfectly to the satisfying harmony between the reddish clay background and the shimmering black-painted areas. The ornamentation is sparing: on the foot the simple halo and at the top a band of lotuses and palmettes to round off the picture. The economy of the picture itself is sparing, too: on the left a palm-tree, on the right the armour, in the middle the little heap of earth and the sword. Grandest and simplest of all, and at the same time extremely bold as an artistic conception, is the rendering of a momentous event just with the one figure of the central character, Ajax. The hero, smitten by Athena with madness, cannot bear his shame after he has returned to his senses, cannot go on living among men. The palm-tree symbolizes the exotic, lonely landscape outside Troy where he fixes his sword upright in the earth and prepares to commit suicide. All the tragic elements embodied by Sophokles in his drama are present in the fateful picture. To the quite unprejudiced beholder of today it is scarcely credible that the picture on the vase was painted before the performance of Sophokles' play, yet it is roughly a hundred years older! Exekias' picture seems like an illustration of Sophokles' verses because it is grounded in a related artistic conception and in the same depth of experience.

In Sophokles, Ajax pretends that he wants to bury his sword on the lonely shore so that no eye can see it any longer:

> For from the hour I gat
> This gift from Hector, my arch-enemy,
> Never one boon, from Argives, did I gather . . .

And he does bury it. But he does not hide it in the earth. He buries it upright with the point upward, so that the blade sticks out of the earth. Ready now to fall on the sword, he begins his last speech in Sophokles' drama with these words:

> Now he stands fast, my executioner;
> Most trenchant so—if there were leisure left
> To reason about it; being, first, Hector's gift,
> The most unwelcome foeman to my sight
> And worst detested; he is fixed, besides,
> In hostile soil, the Troad; newly edged
> Upon the whetting-stone that feeds on steel;
> And I myself fixed him, and set him well,
> Of my quick death the officious instrument!
> So we are ready . . .'*

The same tragic atmosphere plays round the bent, muscular figure of Ajax, who seems to be concentrating so intensely on what he is doing. In the technical sphere the expressive possibilities of the black-figure style have been expanded to such an extent by Exekias that deep wrinkles of worry on the Aeginetan hero's brow are indicated by incised lines. We shall show in a moment how in every respect Exekias exploits to the full the possibilities of the black-figure technique. It remains characteristic of him and his art that even in his later works he favours, out of all the various vase shapes, the strong, tall amphora with its clean, unified outline as the field of activity particularly suited to him.

Exekias repeatedly painted the mighty Ajax dragging the corpse of Achilles out of battle. He assumes in the beholder the knowledge that Ajax will never possess Achilles' weapons. Even this quiet picture has its dramatic tension and contains a tragic conflict.

Amasis Amasis has no trace of any such affinity to tragic drama. His art is related to that of Kleitias. His pictures do not possess the firmness of composition shown by those of Exekias. Frequently they give the effect of more or less fortuitous excerpts from a longer frieze. He likes to put two figures opposite each other; or else he emphasizes

---

* Sir George Young, *The Dramas of Sophocles*, Cambridge-London, 1888, p. 97.

Ajax prepares to kill himself. Amphora by Exekias. About 540 B.C. *Boulogne-sur-Mer*.
Cf. pp. 151, 158, 181.

Clay plate by the painter Lydos. Before the middle of the 6th century B.C. *Munich, Antikensammlungen.*
Cf. pp. 115, 147.

154

one figure in the middle of a group of several figures. Yet his compositions are in no sense action pictures like those of Exekias—whether we are talking of outward or psychological events—but 'situation' pictures. It is true that there is more movement in them when they show Dionysos and his retinue. He is particularly fond of Bacchic scenes. But other gods, too, besides Dionysos, are depicted again and again by Amasis and these gods live in a world where the fate of men does not worry them very much. Here, too, there is a contrast with Exekias, who is particularly concerned with the struggles and difficulties of the legendary heroes and the tragic destiny of men. An oil-jug recently discovered during the excavations PLATE P. 156 in the Kerameikos at Athens is not signed. The subject of the picture is Dionysos, in a long chiton, with a cloak draped over his shoulders and the upper parts of his arms; in his left hand he holds his special drinking vessel, the kantharos. Joyful dancers surround him, one of them with a half-empty wine skin over his shoulder. The style in which the figures are drawn and also the frieze of buds on the shoulder of the vase are so clearly painted by the brush of Amasis that the vase can confidently be ascribed to him.

As far as we know, Amasis signed vases only as potter. Eight of these signed vases have come down to us; they include amphorae with necks that meet the body at a sharp angle and have almost horizontal shoulders, so-called neck-amphorae, and four jugs with trefoil mouths. All these vases look as if they were painted by one and the same painter; it is possible, perhaps even probable, that the potter painted his own vases, as Exekias did, but there is naturally no inscription to prove it. But the painter of the eight vases has had a far greater number of unsigned vases ascribed to him on stylistic grounds. If we assume that potter and painter were identical, then Amasis also painted ordinary amphorae, cups, oil-flasks, small clay implements and beakers. But amphorae seem best suited to his kind of figures and to his mode of composition. On them he employed the compositional principle of putting figures in rows, most clearly to be seen in sculpture in the group of statues FIG. 17 by Geneleos. When the pictures deal with the wine-god Dionysos and the activities of his followers, the Maenads and Satyrs,

Dionysos and Maenads. Neck-amphora by Amasis. About 540 B.C. *Height 13 in. Paris, Bibliothèque Nationale. Cf. pp. 155, 157, 158, 181.*

there are often attempts at a centralized composition; however, they are not really action pictures. This can best be seen on his masterpiece, an amphora with the signature 'Amasis made it', in the Cabinet des Médailles in Paris. On the left stands Dionysos, dignified, clad in a long robe, his big drinking vessel in his right hand, his left hand raised as if in greeting. Before him are two Maenads, who move, embracing each other tightly, in the same rhythm of the dance; one holds a woodland animal, probably a rabbit, which she has grasped by the ears with her right hand. The quiet flow of the measured movements seems to correspond wonderfully with the gentle curve of the vase's shape, and even better with the springy lines of the big free-hand spirals round the handles. The decisive element in the total impression is the specifically ornamental character of the vase. This is of course strengthened by the carefully executed ornaments on the foot and neck, and also by the frieze on the shoulders, which depicts warriors, split up into separate pairs of combatants. As a piece of decorative pottery the amphora by Amasis is superior; on the amphora by Exekias the idea, the content of the picture, has greater weight. PLATE P. 156

People have wondered whether the harmonious, sensitive, ornamental style of Amasis does not reflect Ionian traits and it has even been suggested that Amasis might have been an Ionian artist who had settled in Athens. But to answer these questions we have only to look at an Ionian amphora of similar shape and of about the same time. First of all, the technique is different, the figures are not painted on the clay ground but on a light-coloured slip. As for the pictures themselves, here, too, there is a big difference between these wild figures, with their almost weightless way of moving, and the restrained vivacity of Amasis' figures. It is true that the two vases show some affinity in the ornamental impression that they both produce, but what finally differentiates Amasis' amphora from the Ionian pot with the joyfully dancing drinkers is that decisive clarity of form which characterized Attic vase-painting so clearly even in the Geometric age. Amasis' work has this same quality and in full measure. APPX. PL. 16

The gap between the attitudes of Amasis and Exekias to the content of the picture comes out particularly clearly in the different significance which the elements framing the figures have in the work of PLATE P. 153 each painter. Thus on the amphora in Boulogne the palm-tree which characterizes the landscape is paralleled on the right by the weapons which Ajax has laid to one side and which lean against the edge of the picture. Palm and weapons round off the design formally, but they are also part of its content: they hint at the lonely dialogue between man and nature. The helmet which lies on the top of the shield turns its sightless eye-holes toward the muscular figure in the centre of the picture, who is fully absorbed by what he is doing. The palmettes below the handles, on the other PLATE P. 156 hand, which frame the Dionysiac picture on the amphora by Amasis in Paris are completely different in character. Yet they too form part of the content: they make the figures look less objective and incorporate them firmly in the splendidly devised ornamental system.

Amasis' gods, who confront each other like polite aristocrats, using few gestures, carefully dressed and barbered, frequently seem to be engaged in worldly conversation. The Homeric gods, who enjoy in happy agelessness an easier life than earthly men, found their supreme incarnation in the statues of the sculptor Praxiteles. The figures of Amasis are no less important forerunners of Praxiteles' gods. Thus this tradition extends from Homer through Amasis down to Praxiteles, with an interval of two hundred years between each of the three.

If one wishes to cast a glance from Attica over the other regions of Greece and their vase-painting in the second half of the sixth century, Amasis provides a much better starting point than Exekias. The decorative arrangement of Amasis' figures in the divine dialogues on Olympus, which are like a sort of 'sacra conversazione', and the lively composition of his Bacchic scenes, the 'conversazione profana', are relatively close to contemporary Ionian vase-paintings, while Exekias has nothing comparable to show. The most important of the Ionian potteries was at Chalcis on the island of Euboea. We *Chalcidian vases* know this because the inscriptions on the vases it produced are in the Chalcidian alphabet and fragments of this kind of ware have

Dionysos and komasts. Lekythos by Amasis. 550–540 B.C. *Athens, Kerameikos Museum. Cf. p. 155.*

been found in Chalcis itself. From a chronological point of view, the Chalcidian vases represent a continuation of the Corinthian series. Their earliest attested appearance dates from the very point in time at which the mythological pictures of the so-called Middle Corinthian phase stop. Even the distribution of the inscriptions on the pictures of the Chalcidian artists and the flow of the script are strongly reminiscent of the words on the Corinthian vases. The oldest products of this Chalcidian workshop were possibly made a little earlier than the middle of the sixth century. A vase with a

PLATE P. 162 lid, now in the Würzburg Museum, a so-called column krater, which was used for mixing wine and water and which can serve here as a characteristic example of this kind of vessel, is to be put a little later, in the decade 540–530 B.C. Our illustration shows the back of the vase. It demonstrates the ability of the Chalcidian painters to depict scenes full of lively movement as well. When one

PLATE P. 70 compares the horses on this krater with the quietly walking animals of the early Archaic tradition, which are always of the same type, one sees how expressively these artists have managed to depict races run at full gallop. The front of the same vase bears a scene full of controlled dignity; it takes place at the Trojan royal court. Hector is taking leave of his wife; Paris and Helen are also present. The inscriptions giving the names of the individual characters leave no doubt that a scene from legend is intended. On the other hand, it is probably preferable to interpret the picture on the back as one from daily life rather than as one from myth.

We have already said that in comparison with Chalcidian products the potters and painters of the other Ionian regions have no continuous succession of good-quality creations to show. But this only makes the masterpieces which appear spontaneously and very rarely in these areas, too, during the second half of the sixth century all the more remarkable. Particularly worthy of note is a series of

Ionian 'Little Masters' drinking-cups decorated in the best black-figure technique and produced on Samos. The delicacy of the incised details in their pictures is unparalleled in the whole of Greek vase-painting. Likewise on Samos, but also on the more southerly and bigger Dorian island of Rhodes, a few vases of quite outstanding quality were produced, but their creators prefer the Ionian technique of reservation and only adopt the black-figure technique with considerable hesitation. These vessels are known as Fikellura vases, after the place where they were first discovered. In the matter of shape the Fikellura potters prefer the neck-amphora, and so far as motifs are concerned the painters choose as far as possible those which are decoratively effective. Many of the vases are covered all over with a lozenge pattern consisting of dotted lines, but even those whose main decoration is a figure picture also display an abundance of scrolls and bands on the body.

Fikellura vases

The representative example of this species of vase is an amphora in the museum at Altenburg, on which a group of joyous drinkers is depicted performing a lively dance. The history of this theme can be followed as it develops in the sixth century. It has two roots, one in mythology and the other in everyday life. With the appearance of Sileni in Greek vase-painting, namely in pictures by Sophilos, the depiction of the ecstatic activities of Dionysos' retinue in the so-called Bacchic thiasos has become a favourite theme. Sileni and Maenads take part in the thiasos; Dionysos himself is not always present. The thiasos is one source of the riotous procession of human drinkers, the komos; the Sileni are the forerunners of the komasts. The other source are pictures of the communal feast, at which the participants lie on couches and celebrate the symposium. Just as in real life such feasts can end in drunken revelry in the streets and squares of the city, so the pictures of feasts and the Dionysian dances of the Sileni and Maenads gave rise to the pictures of drinkers enjoying themselves in a relaxed mood. The first examples of such pictures are furnished by some Attic painters, contemporaries of Sophilos. Sir John Beazley has christened them *komast-painters*. On a somewhat later group of Attic vases decorated with friezes, the so-called Tyrrhenian amphorae, it is possible to observe the transition from pictures of the thiasos with its Sileni and Maenads to pictures of human komasts.

APPX. PL. 16

The development of these types of picture, as described here, forms the background to the frieze of komasts on the Fikellura amphora in Altenburg. But it can certainly be maintained that no earlier painter

Horse race. Picture on the back of a Chalcidian lidded krater. Third quarter of 6th century B.C. *Height of vase 16³/₅ in. Würzburg, Martin von Wagner-Museum. Cf. pp. 38, 160.*

has depicted carefree, drunken revelling so congenially as this one; and none is so far removed from the heroic ethos and mythological pictures of the Corinthians, the Chalcidians and Exekias.

Yet even Exekias did not confine himself to the toils of the heroes. Dionysos himself, the favourite figure among the gods of Amasis, was given his most magical treatment by Exekias. It is true that he looks quite different from the Dionysos of Amasis; the whole pictorial conception is different. The picture, on the inside of a cup, was painted some ten years after the Ajax and Maenad amphorae and is still more strongly permeated by the feeling for landscape than the picture of Ajax. A ship moves gently on the sea, driven by a full sail, with dolphins playing round about. In the ship lies the god of wine, stretched out and larger than life. Vines, likewise larger than life, grow up behind the mast; their branches, laden with grapes, hang high over the yard. In his right hand the god holds a drinking-horn. There is no hand at the tiller, but the ship's bow finds its way safely through the ocean: a mid-day epiphany of Dionysos on the high seas.

Exekias' middle period

PLATE P. 164

Colour contrasts play a big part in the composition. Only a few remnants of the once gleaming white of the sail are left, it is true, and unfortunately the original lines of the face have not been preserved. Older reproductions show modern over-painting in this spot; new photographs show only plaster patches similar in shade to the reddish ground of the vase. In any case this picture, for all the mastery of the composition of the scene within the round frame of the vase's lip, edged with black on the inside, is not so much a rendering of an outward action as one of an inward concentration. This same capacity of Exekias for inward concentration is demonstrated by a further work, only a little later, again on an amphora. The right-hand figure—according to the names written on the vase—is Ajax, the left-hand one Achilles. There is a certain similarity to the older picture of Ajax in the way the picture is framed: on the left leans the shield of Achilles, on the right the shield and helmet of Ajax. This time, however, the empty helmet is looking not at the middle of the picture but at the side of the tent—for obviously the scene takes place inside a tent in the camp outside

PLATE P. 166

163

Sea voyage of Dionysos. Picture on the inside of a cup by Exekias. About 530 B.C. *Munich, Antiken-sammlungen. Cf. p. 163.*

Troy. The two heroes are playing some game such as draughts; they are holding their spears in their hands, for no sudden enemy attack must find them unprepared. Yet they are so absorbed in the game, which they accompany with brief exclamations, that they no longer pay attention to any possible danger. Each of the two is concentrating completely on winning the game. In creations like this Exekias is a master of the 'mood picture'; there is no one to touch him in this respect in the whole of antiquity, either before him or after him. This is true of another picture besides the one of Ajax and Achilles, namely the scene on the back of the amphora in the Vatican. It shows 'life in the family circle'; the scene depicted could be imagined taking place in the courtyard of the house of a well-to-do citizen of Athens. These figures on the back of the 'draughts-players' vase are demythologized even more decidedly than those of Ajax and Achilles, yet the figures represent—according to the names by them—the Dioskouroi, Kastor and Polydeukes, and their parents, Leda and Tyndareus. But we are not in a heroic atmosphere here. The picture is at its most impressive at the two spots where man and animal are put side by side; one could almost speak of a spiritual understanding. In the one case Tyndareus is gently stroking the head of a horse; and in the other Polydeukes is bending down to play with a dog, which leaps up at him joyfully. Perhaps the change-over from the black-figure to the red-figure technique, which certainly first appears about 530 B.C., had already begun in Athens, even if at first there were only isolated examples of it at the time when this amphora was made. At any rate, the exceptionally fine use of incision on the cloaks and weapons of the two heroes playing draughts seems to indicate that the painter wishes to use every possible means to justify and maintain his own technique against the newly introduced method of drawing lines on the clay ground with a little brush or bristle. The earliest red-figure vases have been very convincingly compared with battle scenes on the frieze of the Siphnian Treasury at Delphi, which was built shortly before 524 B.C. So far as free-standing sculpture is concerned, a comparison of the Leda in Exekias' Dioskouroi picture with a marble kore from the Acropolis has produced the same date.

Art in the time of the sons of Peisistratos

PLATE P. 168

SCULPTURE

APPX. PL. 17

Achilles and Ajax playing a game similar to draughts. Amphora by Exekias. About 530 B.C. *Height 2 ft. Vatican Museums. Cf. pp. 163 ff.*

This particular figure is therefore often spoken of as the 'Exekias kore'.

This statue of a girl, preserved in its original height, is smaller than life-size. It differs from late Archaic korai mainly in dress. This girl, too, is clad in a chiton, but it only becomes visible at the elbows and over the feet; everywhere else it is hidden by the peplos worn over it. Owing to this arrangement of the clothing there are scarcely any folds; the whole figure is like a solid block. Most of the other korai wear as their main item of clothing a chiton with fine folds in it, and over that an obliquely draped cloak, which is fastened on the right shoulder and likewise produces a complicated series of folds. It has already been shown that this type of kore hails from Ionia, and this type of dress is also an Ionian costume. In addition, as was the tradition in Ionia, the rhythm imparted to the surface by the folds is further enlivened by the gesture of the hand clutching the drapery and pulling it up gently over the ankle. The active hand is almost always the right hand. Accordingly the older korai, down to the thirties of the sixth century, usually pull up their dresses with their right hands. But if the hand holds, say, an animal, a bird, or a fruit, this is the main gesture and it is carried out with the right hand; then the gesture of clutching the dress becomes secondary and is therefore carried out with the left hand. This type of movement is the usual one in the last decades of the sixth century. The Exekias kore, on the other hand, does not touch her dress at all. In her lowered right hand she originally held an object made of metal, probably a garland; her left hand stretched forward at right angles and it, too, originally held something. The lower part of the left arm was made separately, as was usual with a pose like this, and today most of it is lost. Originally this outstretched arm must have made an important contribution to the three-dimensional appearance of the statue. Another factor that originally lent stronger accents to the figure's simple forms was the colouring. Relatively clear traces of colour are still visible even today on the eyes and mouth, on the hair, on the hem of the clothing and as an ornamental pattern on the surface of the clothing. These remnants of colour are partly responsible for the statue's life-like effect, though this is

Hera and Athena in the battle with the giants. From the frieze of the Siphnian Treasury. Marble. Before 525 B.C. *Height 2 ft. Delphi Museum. Cf. pp. 165, 169.*

mainly due to the direct, vital expression of the face, the 'speaking features' of the countenance.

It has been suggested that the name of the creator of the Exekias kore is known, and that the same Attic sculptor, Endoios by name, worked on the north and east friezes of the Treasury of the Siphnians at Delphi. The evidence adduced is not sufficient to prove this thesis, but it is by no means impossible. The Siphnian Treasury and the kore are at any rate virtually contemporaneous. It is obvious that two different workshops were employed on the Treasury reliefs. The pediment and the south and west friezes clearly bear an Ionian stamp, while the design and execution of the north and east

friezes point to a sculptor from further west, perhaps an Athenian PLATE P. 168
in fact. The most vigorous scenes are on the north side. Their
theme is the battle of the gods with the giants. The sculptor has
displayed considerable virtuosity in building up the figures in
different planes. He is not afraid of overlapping; on the contrary,
it enables him to give vivid expression to the restlessness of the
battle. Athena charges a giant who collapses on to his knees; Zeus'
consort goes on eagerly attacking an already fallen opponent. The
fight is still more violent and merciless where wild animals are
taking part in it. The goddess Kybele's chariot is drawn by lions.
But they are not just draught animals; the lions are attacking a PLATE P. 170
giant, whose head, protected by a Corinthian helmet, is given in
three-quarter view. He is being torn to pieces by one of the mighty
animals, which is biting him in the side. The figures in the frieze
are packed close together or strung out more loosely according to
how the tide of battle surges. On one of the giants' round shields the
sculptor put his signature; the verb, an adverb and the predicate
noun have been preserved, but unfortunately not the name itself.
A story told by Herodotus (3,57) gives a precise date for the construction of the Treasury. Through the proceeds of its mines, which
produced precious metals, the little island of Siphnos had grown
wealthy and therefore planned the Treasury at Delphi. In connection
with their plan the Siphnians asked the Delphic Oracle how long
their wealth was likely to last. They did not at first understand the
enigmatic answer which they were given. The story is told by
Herodotus in connection with events which occurred when Kambyses of Persia was mounting a campaign against Egypt. As this
expedition took place in 524 B.C., the construction of the Treasury
must have occurred before this date. The Siphnians spared nothing
when they put up this building. This is shown not by large dimensions but by the precise and well-proportioned execution of every
detail, and especially by the fact that, at any rate for the reliefs
of the north and east friezes, they engaged an excellent and obviously famous sculptor. The Treasury, which was built on a
terrace, is a perfect example of what a high-quality marble building
looked like in the late Archaic period—one that is not a temple,

A lion in Kybele's team seizes a giant. From the frieze of the Siphnian Treasury. Marble. Before 524 B.C. *Height 2 ft. Delphi Museum. Cf. p. 169.*

and therefore not a sacral building in the proper sense, but a typical official building.

The chief point in which it differs from a temple of the standard form is in the absence of the colonnade. The ground-plan is that of a 'building *in antis*'; that is, two supports stand between extended wall ends, which enclose the porch on each side. In comparison with that of a temple-cella this plan is much more compact. The ratio of 1:2 for the width of the porch to the length of the cella, a ratio which the fully developed temple, whether of the Ionic or Doric order, strives to approach, is replaced in the Siphnian Treasury by the *sectio aurea*. This relatively simple type of building has been enriched by making the supports between the antae neither columns nor pillars but kore statues with an architectural function, in other words, so-called caryatids. It will be readily understood that thanks to the fixed chronological point which we possess in the Siphnian Treasury these caryatids are extremely valuable for the dating of the Acropolis korai, even if they do not belong to those parts of the Treasury's sculptural decorations which we can venture to ascribe to Attic sculptors.

The main temple at the same sanctuary had also been due for rebuilding since the middle of the sixth century. The execution of this plan seems to have continually met fresh difficulties; the

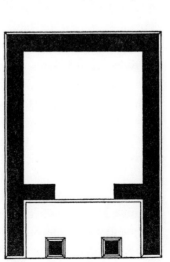

FIG. 33

FIG. 34

FIG. 33 – *Delphi, Siphnian Treasury. About 525 B.C. (P. de La Coste-Messelière, Au Musée de Delphes, 487, Fig. 20).*

171

FIG. 34 – *Delphi, Siphnian Treasury. Reconstruction (P. de La Coste-Messelière, Au Musée de Delphes, 283, Fig. 13).*

decisive one was lack of money, although financial contributions were made by many cities and territories, some of them far distant ones. Nevertheless, a start was made with the preparations. Among these was the architectural strengthening of the big terrace on which the temple was to be erected. Labour and expense were not PLATE P. 174 spared. We are indebted to this project for the finest wall of polygonal blocks that has come down to us from antiquity. In the Argive citadels of the Mycenean age the polygonal cutting and setting of the huge blocks was intended to make the resulting wall particularly firm; and the same purpose can certainly be assumed in the case of the polygonal stone walls of the second millennium B.C. on the

Acropolis of Athens. Solidity was certainly also one of the main aims in the retaining wall for the terrace of the temple of Apollo at Delphi, but here the individual blocks are not huge lumps of limestone, as they were in the prehistoric epoch, but marble, and they are also smaller and cut in a positively elegant fashion. With this technique it was certainly not possible to fit the stones together with such invisible joints as the square blocks in the Periclean buildings on the Acropolis; but the ornamental pattern produced by the joints, with its distant similarity to honeycombs (though much more irregular and therefore rhythmically more effective) brings an almost incredibly complicated architectural technique to its logical conclusion. The visitor to the sanctuary who walks along this retaining wall is prepared for the still more splendid edifice which presumably awaits him on the top of the terrace—the temple. It seems to us, however, that this building did not fulfil all the expectations awakened in this way. It was a long time, it is true, before the construction of the temple itself actually began. This only came to pass in the last decade but one of the sixth century, when the Attic family of the Alkmeonidai, which had been banished from Athens at that time by the tyrants, strove to get back to Athens and to regain their influence on the political destiny of their city by energetically furthering, obviously in a deliberately propagandist way, the rebuilding of the sanctuary of Apollo at Delphi. Only chance fragments of the superstructure of their temple are still preserved, but their enlargement and 'monumentalization' of the whole sanctuary, devastated by a fire in 548 B.C., remained final. Particularly decisive from the point of view of religious history was the partial destruction at that time, in connection with the process of replanning, of old sanctuaries with traditions going back far into the prehistoric period. For example, the retaining wall of polygonal blocks cut through the sanctuary of the earth-goddess and covered up older treasuries. Naturally there were replacements in the new plan for what had been destroyed and the abodes of the old cults were absorbed into the temple of Apollo, which now for PLATE P. 176 the first time dominated the original cults. Thus, not only the site in the heroic landscape of the Pleistos valley, below the steep cliffs

Terrace wall in the precinct of Apollo at Delphi. Third quarter of 6th century B.C. *Cf. pp. 172 ff.*

and by the Kastalian spring, has remained the same since the end of the sixth century; so too has the topographical situation of the sanctuary—the outer walls of the precinct, the retaining wall of the temple terrace, the size and foundations of the temple. The temple itself, however, was completely rebuilt in the fourth century, and all that is left of the sculptural decorations of the Archaic building is a few pedimental sculptures, both from the marble front and the limestone back. These fragments of sculpture are important because they all confirm that the builders of the temple, the Alkmeonidai, entrusted its decoration to an Attic sculptor. Antenor, whom we know from signatures that have been preserved and also as the sculptor of one of the kore statues on the Acropolis, and who was also given state commissions by the young Athenian democracy, *Athens* also made, with his assistants, these pedimental figures. It seems that the builders of the temple aimed at trumping the new temple of Athena erected a short time before on the Acropolis by the sons of Peisistratos. The very choice of theme for the west pediment contained a clear reference to the new Athenian building: on both temples the subject of the relief is the gigantomachy. Probably the composition was also similar, in that on both reliefs there was a caesura exactly in the middle of the pediment: the middle was left empty and the gods' leaders in the battle, Zeus and Athena, fought from there, back to back, facing the corners of the pediment. The east pediment, on the other hand, is the first example of the epiphany of a god being shown on a pediment. In this particular case it is the occupant of the temple himself, Apollo, who appears here in the middle, standing frontally on a chariot. Thus the 'mythical picture', as already exemplified in the Gorgon pediment from Corcyra, is taken up again, but endowed with a meaning which points forward to the epiphanies of Classical art, to the figures of Zeus and Apollo on the pediments of the temple of Zeus at Olympia and to the birth of Athena on the front pediment of the Parthenon.

Yet for all this the remains preserved seem to betray a certain aridity. The creative power does not seem quite up to filling the large spaces involved in a really meaningful way. Indeed, in the execution of the individual sections, some of the older pedimental compositions, such as that of the temple in Corcyra or the two PLATE P. 92 versions of the sculptural decorations of the Archaic temple of Athena on the Acropolis, are more splendid, more inspired. This is probably connected with the phenomenon already mentioned above, namely the real decline in monumental power evident in the late Archaic period, the lack of inner greatness in the figures. How far the temple of Apollo at Eretria in Euboea and its pediment, *Eretria* which showed the abduction of the Amazon Antiope by the Attic hero Theseus, were affected by this same phenomenon it is impossible to say because of the scantiness of the remains. It is to be

Delphi, sanctuary of Apollo. *Cf. pp. 173 f.*

hoped that the new combined Greco-Swiss excavations there will bring to light enough fragments of architecture and sculpture for us to form a better judgement of the building as a whole. In any case, with the temple of Athena on the Acropolis and the temple of Apollo at Delphi, it makes the third major building enterprise of the late Archaic period that was carried out, if not entirely by Athenians, at any rate under strong Attic influence.

The temple of Athena at Paestum, on the other hand, takes us into a completely different geographical area and also into a different artistic atmosphere. Perhaps the very fact that in size it comes a long way behind the temple of Hera, erected about a generation earlier, likewise in Paestum, reveals the realization of its builder that this late period was not the time to create enormous, exaggerated forms. He laid the main emphasis, in both the design and the appearance of this fortunately still well-preserved building, on the finest harmony of the parts and the perfect execution of every detail. The result is that in the architectonic forms 'all violence of expression is absent and likewise all hardness in the appearance of the plastic entity'; they lack monumentality, but in return they are delicate and graceful. They perhaps correspond most in the realm of architecture to what we have described in the other branches of art towards the end of the sixth century as a loss in 'weight' and a gain in ornamental quality. They therefore correspond most in their own field to the sensitive and skilfully modelled achievements of miniature art, in which the late archaic 'fairy-tale world' finds appropriate expression. That this feeling for form could find such perfect expression in a building is partly due to the geographical region in which the conception was turned into reality. From the start the Greeks in the Italian colonies spoke a softer tongue than their compatriots in the mother country. Wealth and enjoyment of life, and also the splendour and charm of artistic creation, characterize the Greek cities on Italian and Sicilian soil. This is their particular contribution to the Hellenic culture and Greek art as a whole, and one that both would be the poorer without.

This temple, built about 510 B.C., is also the earliest example of the mixture—or better, the harmonious combination—of the Doric

PLATE P. 179

Magna Graecia

and Ionic orders. Certain details of the ground-plan and of the entablature, which elsewhere appear only in Ionic buildings, occur here in a building that is in principle, and above all in the outward appearance of the colonnade or peristyle, a Doric one. But the columns which stand directly in front of the cella and belong to its porch are Ionic columns with Ionic capitals. The cella is not of the type usual by this time in the Doric order, that of the double building *in antis*, nor yet a simple building *in antis* like the Treasury of the Siphnians, but a prostyle building; that is, the porch is not entered between two columns, pillars or caryatids standing on the level of the projecting wall ends, i.e. the antae, but through a row consisting altogether of four columns, which stand in front of the correspondingly shortened antae. This type is further enriched in the temple of Athena at Paestum by the fact that the projecting wall ends are not thickened into antae but concealed by directly attached half-columns. Yet another column stands between this half-column and the *prostasis*. The number of columns is in the standard ratio of 6:13.

The magical charm of late Archaic creations becomes most evident in the art of the vase-painters. No one else is better able to lead us into the fairy-tale world of the late Archaic period. Even Exekias forgets, in the pictures he painted in the twenties, the heroic atmosphere of the work he produced in the years of his maturity and mastery. This shows that although he was getting on in years he was still able to adapt himself to new trends. Among his latest works is a mixing-vessel that opens out like a calyx, a 'calyx krater' which was discovered during the excavations by American archaeologists in the market-place of Athens and is now in the Agora Museum there. Over the handles, instead of an ornamental pattern, a figure picture is painted, but one that has an ornamental character. Vines grow up from the handles, as they do from Dionysos' ship on the cup in Munich, and these vines branch out and bear leaves and rich fruit. On one of the slender tendrils of this vine, indeed

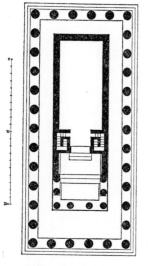

FIG. 35 – *Paestum, temple of Athena. About 510 B.C.*
(F. Krauss, Die Tempel von Paestum, I, 1, Plate 3).

Paestum, temple of Athena. About 510 B.C. *Cf. p. 177.*

on the slenderest of all, sits a nymph, balancing unrealistically, PLATE P. 182 rocking as though in a dream.

Already on the weapons and cloaks of the heroes playing draughts in the tent outside Troy Exekias had attempted to attain by means of abundant, very detailed incisions effects which were obtainable much more easily in the red-figure technique with its finer and, in particular, more pliable tools. This aim is even more clearly perceptible in the clothes of the Scythian archer who adorns the fragment of an amphora in the museum of the University of PLATE P. 189 Philadelphia. The whole figure is clad in a suit covered with ornamental patterns. Across the middle of the body hangs the big quiver. The hands hold the huge, springy bow. A cap covers the head, but the feet are bare. The Scythian archer is also a very popular subject on contemporary red-figure vases. Thus once again Exekias competes against the devotees of the new red-figure mode of painting with an achievement which exhausts the most delicate possibilities of the traditional technique. The late date of the black-figure archer is already attested by two other characteristics, the wonderfully impressive depiction of the way in which the figure edges forward on the soles of the feet and the living, flowing outlines with which the figure is set on the clay background of the picture.

Oltos

PLATE P. 192 A drawing by the early red-figure painter Oltos on an amphora in the British Museum was executed some ten years after the archer. Oltos was able here to make use of the experience and achievements of the first generation of practitioners of the new technique; and he himself had already acquired a certain amount of experience. The very vase on which he painted offers—apart from the stout, three-dimensionally conceived body, with its swinging outline—a new and striking use of the few colours at the painter's disposal. It is not only that the clay-coloured underside of the foot contributes to the colours visible on the standing vase and that the lower dividing band is painted purple; but the handles, straining upward in the polished radiance of the clay colour, on the one hand correspond to the figure standing alone on the metallic black of the vase's surface and on the other stand out as clearly from the body of the vase as if they were made of a completely different material or did not really belong to the vase as a whole!

The single figure on the other side of the amphora is a warrior labelled Achilles. Next to the figure of the girl in Ionian costume— chiton and cloak—the name Briseis is inscribed. In her hair she wears a garland and in her left hand she holds a flower, which she is just raising to her nose, while her narrow, almond-shaped eye gazes with delight at the flower. Briseis has no base-line or platform to support and define her position on the surface of the vase. She hovers like Exekias' nymph in the web of vine-shoots, or rather still more unrealistically than that girl, for there is not even a little branch to hold her up. Yet Oltos' drawing is more comprehensible; it produces a more realistic effect than Exekias' nymph, not a less realistic one. With this kind of decoration Oltos established a new convention which was to be extremely successful in the first few decades of the fifth century. Later painters sometimes considered it necessary to give single figures on a black surface a firm platform in the shape of a line or a strip of ornament. But the new type of picture is made precisely by the contrast between curving background and the clear, objective drawing imposed on it, and its creator knew how to use it in this way with great virtuosity. But if the new kind of decoration as such had a great future before it, this drawing itself is only comprehensible in the context of the magical poetry of the late Archaic period. It was certainly made in the time of the tyrant Hippias, in other words before 510 B.C.

If one recalls at this point the development which this kind of vase, the amphora, had gone through between the late eighth century and the late sixth century, one cannot help being amazed at the variety of possibilities there are in the way of construction, contour and decoration. At the same time the history of this particular form sums up the whole history of Greek art during the period discussed in this book. Our journey has led us from the slender forms which characterize the end of the Geometric period and which are represented by the late Geometric, perhaps somewhat mannered amphora in the Louvre, down to the powerful, expansive, yet stiffly tensed shape of the amphora with the picture of the Polyphemos adventure. Much the same interval of time as that between these two vases also separates the Polyphemos vase from the monumental black-figure funerary amphora from the Peiraieus. It is interesting to compare the horses on the Geometric vase with those on the black-figure one. The pictures—painted at an interval of eighty years—show both the persistence of what is in the last analysis the same type and also the sudden acquisition by the black-figure animals of solidity and a monumental quality. The amphora by Exekias at Boulogne and that by Amasis in the Louvre are eighty years later. The black-figure technique is now at its zenith, so that the pictures on the Peiraieus amphora, seen from this point, can only be regarded as the product of a preliminary phase, perhaps grandiose but also uncanny in their proportions. The vase shape as

History of the development of amphora shapes

APPX. PL. 10
APPX. PL. 11

PLATE P. 70

PLATES PP. 153 AND 156

Nymph amid vine tendrils. Decoration over the handle of a calyx krater by Exekias. 530–520 B.C. *Height of vase 17 in. Athens, Agora Museum. Cf. pp. 178 f.*

such has now split up into the strictly and essentially different types of the ordinary amphora and the neck-amphora. It goes without saying that in both Amasis and Exekias the character of the pictures remains, in accordance with the nature of black-figure art, consistently two-dimensional, that is, flat. Finally, in the amphora by Oltos in the British Museum, which is about thirty years later, there comes, in addition to the vessel's tectonic, which gives the vase a hitherto unparalleled plasticity, the conquest of the artistic realm opened up by the red-figure technique. Now the painted figure, too, seems three-dimensional; it appears like a statue in front of the neutral background of the vase's surface.

PLATE P. 192

Is the assumption justified that during the period of the tyrannies and by this form of government a certain kind of man was produced, in Athens at any rate? It can be regarded as certain that during this period a perceptible amount of Ionian influence can be traced in Attic sculpture and architecture, and that it was favoured by the tyranny. Most of the Acropolis korai are clear examples of this; so is the fact that a big temple of Zeus was planned and begun in the years round 520 B.C. Athens, too, was to have one of these over-sized temples otherwise known only in Ionia; and naturally such a building is only conceivable in the Ionic order of architecture. After the fall of Hippias, in the time of the Athenian democracy, the temple remained unfinished. It was only completed on the initiative of the Emperor Hadrian, and then in the order predominantly employed in the Roman imperial period, the Corinthian. The link between the court of Polykrates of Samos and that of the sons of Peisistratos also deserves to be emphasized. The presence of the lyric poets Ibykos and Anakreon was certainly not without effect on intellectual life at the court of Polykrates. Anakreon came from Samos to Athens, probably after Polykrates was captured and put to death by the Persians. In Athens he belonged, together with the poet Simonides of Keos, to the circle round Hipparchos. The young men of aristocratic birth who belonged to this circle may sometimes have had, in their over-civilized, distinguished behaviour, an affinity with the figures of Amasis, or later may even have been similar to the faintly decadent youths who appear as elegantly

Influence of the form of government on art

183

FIG. 36 – *Inscription on the base of a funerary statue. Marble. About 520–510 B.C. Athens, Kerameikos Museum (Athen. Mitt., 78, 1963, supplement 69, 2).*

PLATE P. 192

dressed spectators and listeners on the amphorae of Andokides. Oltos' Briseis cannot simply be lumped together with these perfumed representatives of the *jeunesse dorée* of the Athens of those days; she was more probably inspired by the competitions between rhapsodes by which the old epics were given fresh life in the musical contests of the Panathenaic festivals. At any rate, the subtle drawing of the figure, the intense gaze from the narrow eye, the holding of the flower to the nose, all express a feeling for life and a code of manners which could best be described as 'courtly' art. One would think that after the expulsion of the tyrants red-figure vase-painting would have changed. People have therefore, with some justice, contrasted with Oltos' pictures 'the new greatness of style of painters like Euphronios and Euthymides'. Such distinctions between art *before* 510, the year of Hippias' fall, and the period *after* that date, when Kleisthenes introduced a new constitution, are not unfounded. In sculpture, too, especially as far as tombs are concerned, people have spoken of a Peisistratid era and a Kleisthenic era. A statue that certainly belonged to the era of the Peisistratidae, that is, the era of Hippias and Hipparchos, is the one that stood on a base, still

FIG. 36   preserved, bearing the inscription: 'Grave of Aischros from Samos, the son of Zoilos.' This base was not found in Samos but in the Athenian cemetery outside the Dipylon gate. Aischros was thus buried in Athens. It is quite possible that he left his native island after the death of Polykrates. He died, then, in the Athens of the Peisistratidae. A sculptor from Samos—this inference is supported by the very fragmentary remains of a statue probably belonging to the base—made his memorial and also carved the inscription on the base in the Samian alphabet. A comparison of this Aischros inscription with the letters of the earlier Attic inscription to Phrasikleia will show the difference between Peisistratan and Peisistratid forms. The ornamental character of the letters in the Aischros inscription brings out the difference clearly. The change in the style of writing shows like a seismograph, a change not only in art but also in the whole cultural structure. FIG. 32

There is a similar chronological relationship between the Exekias kore discussed above and the head of a kore statue which was also found on the Acropolis but because of its style must have been carved some twenty years later. We are now faced with this question: are the forms of this head still a reflection of the last few years of Hippias' régime or do they derive from the time when Athens had already found its own particular form of government, democracy? The change that has taken place in the modelling of the countenance in the interval between the Exekias kore and the isolated head whose special importance was first recognized by Humfry Payne is by no means slight. A much more complicated mentality is now reflected in the features of the face; in comparison the effect of the Exekias kore is much simpler and more direct. Yet the later sculptor's artistic ability is also revealed by the fact that, in spite of the more contrasted, fuller modelling of the details, in the shaping of the surface and in the contours his work possesses just as strong an artistic unity as the Exekias kore. Human nature here is more reserved, quieter, perhaps more conscious of itself than the forthcoming, unreflecting manner of the Exekias kore would have permitted. This special character of the head emerges most clearly when one analyses the modelling of the thick, soft eyelids and the wide mouth, which looks as if it is about to open. These details, expressive and 'full' as they are, 'yet seem'—I repeat Payne's phrase—'so far from being on the surrounding forms, to be their natural conclusion'.

Attic sculpture in the early years of democracy

APPX. PL. 17

APPX. PL. 14

Seen thus, the head seems more easily understood as evidence of the years which also produced the Constitution of Kleisthenes. We should then have to place between the Exekias kore and the head not only other korai from the Acropolis, such as those numbered

PLATE P. 192670, 672 and 673, but also, above all, Oltos' Briseis picture, which, although it is further away in time, has more of the Exekias kore in its nature than of the later head. Such a chronological arrangement FIG. 37 is also supported by Attic reliefs of this period. First of all there is a monumental base, which again comes from the cemetery in the Kerameikos and originally bore a grave statue. On the three carved sides of this base there are sporting scenes—a game with a ball, wrestling, javelin-throwing—and a picture of four young men watching with interest the hostility which is developing between a cat and a dog. These reliefs do not possess quite the artistic quality of the kore head just discussed, but the formal idiom is the same. The Archaic scheme of putting the individual forms alongside each other is gradually yielding to the idea of subordinating the individual details to a dominating total concept. This reflects a mental attitude which is certainly not so uncomplicated as the Archaic attitude, but instead is approaching the moment of individual self-knowledge when the problems not only exist in artistic creation as a threat to a formal tradition but are also present in the mind of the artist.

The rendering of the folds in these reliefs enables us to follow these characteristic forms, as well as what they express, into the next phase of development and from one branch of art to another. Just as human personality and its depiction could be followed from the Exekias kore to the Briseis of Oltos, from there to the kore head and again from there to the base of the grave statue, so this development

Vase-painting in the early years of democracy is brought to a conclusion by a vase-painting which may be regarded as the swan song of the history of Archaic art. Already in his earliest paintings, which date from the last decade of the sixth century and probably the early part of it, Euphronios had overcome a certain preciosity which marks the Archaic style, including both the late works of Amasis and Exekias and also the red-figure vases of Ando- PLATE P. 195 kides, Epiktetos the Elder and Oltos. In a vase-painting that may have been made in the fifth century, this achievement is combined with a curious, almost faintly oppressive stillness, indeed something like a touch of melancholy.

The painting in question consists of a not very large number of sherds which, when fitted together, form part of a pictorial frieze

FIG. 37 – *Extract from the reliefs on the base of a sepulchral monument. Marble. After 510 B.C. Athens, National Museum.*

on the outside of a drinking-cup. On the right some letters are preserved; they are the end of the signature with which Euphronios signed the cup as painter. Above, in front of the profile of a face only the lower part of which is still visible, is the inscription 'Thetis'. This indicates the theme: the sea-goddess Thetis being led home as his bride by Peleus. This is no forceful abduction like the one portrayed by Euthymides in his picture of Korone being carried off by Theseus, on an amphora in the Munich collection of vases, or by the sculptor who, on the pediment from Eretria, shows Antiope being carried off by the same Theseus. Instead, we see here slow, hesitating steps and restrained gestures. It may be that the loss of the upper part of the frieze makes the beholder try all the harder to understand the picture; but as a result the characteristic features become all the more quickly and easily perceptible to the eye. On the left the chariot to which Peleus is leading Thetis stands ready to start. Other, long-robed figures become visible. On the right there is a narrow double line—probably a spear held slantwise. The particular mood of the picture is summed up in the attitude of the bridal pair's hands. Peleus has grasped Thetis by the wrist with his left hand, but the outspread fingers reveal how loose and gentle his grip is. And Thetis stretches out not only the fingers of this hand held by Peleus in the direction which all the figures and the chariot are taking, but also the forefinger and middle finger of her left hand. On her left forearm she wears a bracelet wound round two or three times. The ornamental band of horizontal palmettes which serves as a base or platform for the picture also deserves attention, fragmentary though it is now.

The shape of the palmette-leaves in this ornamental band looks slightly more old-fashioned than the leaves of the three palmettes in the segment of a round picture on the inside of a drinking-cup PLATE ON SLIP-CASE which may be the last vase painted by Euphronios. This cup is signed by Sosias, as potter; the signature of Euphronios is still found on later vases, but in each case in the form of a potter's signature. The picture on the inside of the cup by Sosias speaks of a new relationship between man and man. It is not by chance that this relationship appears in a picture which shows one warrior helping another, a younger man helping an older one—Achilles binding up the wounds of Patroklos. The way in which here all the minute details are given but emphatically subordinated to the theme of the picture as a whole provides evidence of the hitherto unknown possibilities of a composition consisting of physical and spiritual elements combined in perfect harmony. The moving bodies are understood as organic forms acting meaningfully; look, for example, at the legs, sharply bent at the knee, or at Patroklos' foot, planted against the frame of the picture. On the other hand, the shield which is lying on the ground and on which Patroklos sits gives the composition solidity. The propping movement of Patroklos' right

Scythian archer. Fragments of an amphora by Exekias. 530–520 B.C. *Philadelphia, University Museum.* Cf. *p. 179.*

189

hand, his bowed, averted head and his open mouth, Achilles' gaze, anxiously fixed upon the bandage—these formal devices give the picture not only atmosphere but also psychological concentration. And in this concentration there is a new awareness. Atmosphere, which was indissoluble from the picture's content and from the treatment of the theme, was already present in the mature compositions of Exekias. But this atmosphere was self-evidently inherent in the pictures; it was simply present and raised no problems. With the appearance of man's awareness of his actions, a hitherto unfelt sense of responsibility comes to life. That this feeling can now be taken for granted marks a contrast between these pictures and their predecessors. Really they no longer belong to the Archaic world. This raises in a more pressing form the question whether this change has anything to do with the end of the tyranny and the establishment of the Athenian democracy.

Persian Wars Up to fifty years ago these changes, and likewise the dividing line between Greek Archaic art and Greek Classical art, were regarded as conditioned by the events of the Persian Wars. The immeasurable threat to Greece posed by the Persians and the unexpectedly successful resistance of the Hellenes to this hostile super-power were supposed to have called forth the earnestness of early Classical art, with its simultaneously strict and free forms, the ethical evaluations of the dramatists and the national consciousness of the Greeks. Then, later on, an attempt was made to see the Persian Wars and the events connected with them rather as a symptom than as a cause of the new dimensions of form and spirit. Today we are perhaps inclined in the same way to see the changed political and social structures, too, as symptoms and to try to trace them back to deeper, not obviously perceptible causes. But did the change in form of government at Athens, deeply as it affected the life of the individual Athenian, really mean a decisive alteration in structure, a revolution, for the whole of Greece?

Continuity between Athenian politics and history of Archaic art This question can confidently be answered in the negative. Even for the city of Athens and the Attic countryside the result of Kleisthenes' Constitution should not be regarded as a complete and final break with all previous development. The life of the Greek city-states had not flowed on in uneventful peace during the sixth century even before the establishment of the Athenian democracy, least of all in Athens. Yet in this period the course of history, and not only Athenian history, gives an impression of logical consistency and almost seems to be working towards a predetermined goal. Many of the ideas latent in Solon's Constitution, which, since they required the prior execution of other reforms could not be put into practice at the beginning of the sixth century, were turned into reality by Peisistratos. For example, it was he who secured the final liberation of the rural population, by means of a distribution of land; at the same time the obligation to give up a sixth of their yield was lifted from the shoulders of those small farmers who had had to pay this interest up till then. Kleisthenes now moved further along the same path by granting citizenship to a large number of resident aliens who previously had not possessed it. Here, too, he was moving in the same direction as Solon. The same consistent policy extending over a long period of time can also be observed in the realm of cultural organization. The Panathenaic festival was founded six years before Peisistratos' *coup d'état*, but the tyrant developed it further, particularly the contests of musicians and rhapsodes; and of course even after Hippias and right through the Periclean age the Panathenaea was the central event in the Attic calendar. It is true that the division of the whole population into the ten new *phylai*, the organizational mixing of rural and urban citizens and the introduction of ostracism were all complete innovations that came in with the democracy and touched the very roots of society. Yet even with these innovations one has the impression that they represent the conclusion of a process of thought that had gone on in the minds of the Athenians for some time and was simply made generally visible by the Constitution of Kleisthenes. If that had not been the case Kleisthenes as a single individual would never have been able to get these innovations adopted, not even with the support of the whole family of the Alkmeonidai.

So much for the fundamentally unified development of politics and art in Archaic Athens. So far as local variants and the autonomous individuality of the various regions of Greece are concerned, it must

Art, politics and religion

be said at once that, although since 630 B.C. the artistic energies of Greece had been centred on Athens as if at a sort of focal point, the city nevertheless—or perhaps precisely because of this—gradually became more and more the typical representative, the exemplary model, of almost all Greek cities. Of course, this assertion does not contradict the numerous structural differences that we have noted again and again in the foregoing pages. It is simply that the rhythm of development and the succession of individual stylistic phases is the same in all regions. This is true even of political phenomena. For example, although in the sixth century there were tyrannies only in certain areas—the best example outside Athens and Samos is Naxos, where Polykrates' ally Lygdamis ruled—yet, from a more general point of view, political and cultural ambitions and the various ways of achieving them were not fundamentally different from those of the tyrants. In particular, first through the complete uniformity of religion, always coming to the fore through the great sporting festivals at the supra-regional sanctuaries, and secondly under the influence of the many different aristocratic families, whether states were ruled by tyrannies or not, the Greeks developed a national consciousness which was then able to resist the Persian attack and but for which—a little later—Pindar and Sophokles, Pheidias and Polykleitos would be unimaginable.

At this point we must draw the reader's attention once again, with some emphasis, to a loosening up of mythological and religious forms which the contemplation of the works of art discussed above has already brought to our notice. This can be equated with the spread of the cult of Dionysos and its taking root in the religious experience of all classes of the population. These events took place in the sixth century. Clear evidence of this is provided by the Dionysiac pictures favoured especially by the Attic vase-painters and the portraits of Dionysos himself. A fixed chronological point for the establishment of this movement is finally provided by the

Religion and philosophy

Amphora by the potter Euxitheos; the picture of Briseis was painted by Oltos. About 510 B.C. *London, British Museum. Cf. pp. 180, 183, 184, 186.*

addition of theatrical performances to the worship of Dionysos and by the construction of the temple of Dionysos at Athens, in the twenties of the sixth century.

Philosophic or mystic currents like the Orphic cult and the teaching of Pythagoras, elaborated in the last few decades of the sixth century, are at least related to the cult of Dionysos and were to have a considerable influence on late Archaic art, particularly that of southern Italy. On the other hand, Herakleitos, who was probably born only a few years after Pythagoras, can no longer be described as one of the last thinkers of Archaic Greece. So far as the few fragments handed down to us allow us to understand his doctrine of spiritual tensions, of antinomies, his philosophy leads rather into the dramatic tension of the fifth century. His logical move from Ionian natural philosophy to metaphysics is the conscious decision of a post-Archaic mind. For 'the thing in itself', matter, substance belong to the realm of Archaic thought. So in a similar way does the mysterious origin of matter. Neither the former nor the latter is essentially transcendent; everything is nature.

Nature and art

Two reservations must be added to this, or rather not so much reservations as qualifications. This nature can never be formless. It certainly expresses itself in complete simplicity, but only in clear form. Just as the Greeks saw mountain and forest, sea and river, as inhabited by concrete beings, so nature in every one of its manifestations possesses form, and the form of a work of art. Stylization in Archaic art is stricter than in any other artistic period. At the same time there is a constant tendency to simplify, to make do with few types. This makes the ensuing artistic creations all the weightier, all the more powerful and impressive.

Second—and this is really already contained in the definition, for the object is part of nature—matter is never dead matter, but is always felt as full of life; it radiates life. Spiritual life is incorporated in matter when it is given artistic form. Through this spiritual life even unfeeling nature acquires sublimity.

In the three centuries which we have traversed the content and form of Archaic art were subject to changes. The strictest Geometric stylization characterizes the four-sided framed picture between the

PLATE P. 13

Peleus abducts Thetis. Picture on the outside of a drinking-cup painted by Euphronios. About 500 B.C. *Height of pictorial frieze 5 in. Athens, National Museum. Cf. pp. 186 f.*

handles of the monumental grave amphora. The sinister experience of uncontrolled impulse, bloodthirstiness and death which the Greeks went through during the revolutions of the seventh century— to the very brink of self-destruction—is reflected in animal pictures PLATE P. 59 like the one on the shoulder of a Corinthian jug. This experience is intensified still further in the wild demonic quality of the Gorgon of APPX. PL. 18 Corcyra, and at the same time is overcome by enclosing the instinctive powers of terror between the worlds of the Olympian gods and the Homeric heroes. In the central group of a pediment which must have belonged to a very small building on the Acropolis APPX. PL. 19 another fight between animals is depicted. With it Archaic art comes to an end. For the theme is no longer the supernatural wildness of the lion, as on the Corinthian jug, nor the awe-inspiring demonic quality peculiar to the Gorgon on the pediment from Corcyra, but a sort of *natural* wildness, which makes us see the death of the bull calf only as part of a very much more comprehensive, but ordered series of events, ordered according to the laws of organic life. At this stage in art a tragic scene like this even participates in this harmony, this new tranquillity of existence, in the equilibrium of life and death. Classical art is at hand.

APPENDICES

CHRONOLOGICAL TABLE

Date		History	Architecture, Sculpture, Relief
	926	Destruction of Tell Abu Hawam in Palestine	
800			
			Heraion I on Samos
750		Foundation of Cumae	
			Small bronzes, terracottas
	735	Foundation of Syracuse	
	740–20	1st Messenian War	
	708	Foundation of Tarentum	Ivory finds in the palace of Sargon II
	722–05	Sargon II of Assyria	at Nimrud
700			
	690	Foundation of Gela	Sphyrelata
			Heraion II on Samos
	660–40	2nd Messenian War	
650			
			Start of large-scale stone sculpture on the Cyclades and in Attica
	c. 636	Kylon's *coup d'état* at Athens	
	628	Foundation of Selinus	
	621	Drakon's legislation at Athens	Later temple of Apollo at Thermon
		Kypselos tyrant of Corinth	
600			
		Periander tyrant of Corinth	
	594	Solon's archonship at Athens	Temple of Artemis in Corfu
			Limestone pediments of the older temples on the Acropolis at Athens
			'Rhoikos temple' in Samos (Heraion III)
	561–60	Peisistratos' *coup d'état* at Athens	Theodoros of Samos, architect and
550			bronze-caster
	560–47	Kroisos King of Lydia	Geneleos, sculptor
			Temple of Artemis at Ephesos
			Temple of Apollo at Corinth
	from 538	Polykrates sole ruler in Samos	Sculptors: Endoios
	c. 540–25	Lygdamis tyrant of Naxos	Aristokles
	528–27	Death of Peisistratos	Antenor
	522	Death of Polykrates	before 525 Treasury of Siphnians at Delphi
	514	Murder of Hipparchos by Harmodios and Aristogeiton	
			Completion of the older temple of Apollo at Delphi
	510	Hippias driven into exile	
	508	Kleisthenes' reforms at Athens	
500			

CHRONOLOGICAL TABLE

Pottery, Painting	Cultural History	Date
Protogeometric pottery at Tell Abu Hawam		
		800
Attic ripe Geometric style	776 Start of the Olympic victors' lists	
Start of the early Protocorinthian style		750
	Homeric epics: Iliad	
Attic late Geometric style		
	Odyssey	
		700
1st black-figure style at Corinth (middle Protocorinthian)	Hesiod	
Early Attic Nessos amphora in New York		
	Tyrtaios	
1st black-figure style at Athens		
		650
	Archilochos of Paros	
Late Protocorinthian (Chigi jug)		
	624 Thales of Miletos born	
620–10 Start of Corinthian style	611 Anaximander of Miletos born	
Black-figure Nessos amphora in Athens	Alkaios and Sappho of Mytilene	
		600
Attic vase painters: Corinth:		
Gorgon painter Timonidas		
Sophilos		
	586 Anaximenes born	
	585 Eclipse of the sun, predicted by Thales	
	580 Pythagoras born	
Kl(e)itias & Ergotimos	570 Xenophanes born	
	566 Establishment of the Great Panathenaia	
Oldest Panathenaic amphorae	at Athens	
Lydos Nearchos		
		550
Amasis Attic Little Masters	Anakreon of Teos	
Exekias		
	Simonides of Keos	
530 Introduction of red-figure technique	534 First performance of tragedy at Athens (Thespis)	
Andokides painter		
Psiax		
Oltos Epiktetos		
Euthymides Euphronios	510–500 Ephebe period of Leagros and	
Large-scale painting: Kimon of Kleonai	Themistokles	
		500

CAPTIONS TO APPENDIX OF PLATES

('Appx. pl.' in the margin of the text refers to the following plates.)

1 – Early Archaic Cycladic amphora: detail showing grazing stag. About 650 B.C. Height of vase 23 in. Stockholm, National Museum. Arias-Hirmer-Shefton, History of Greek Vase-Painting, Fig. 25. *Cf. p. 37.*

2/3 – Ivory figure of a kneeling youth, part of an implement (cf. Fig. 11). About 630 B.C. Height 5³/₅ in. Athens, National Museum. E. Buschor, Altsamische Standbilder, IV, Figs. 241/242. Reconstruction: D. Ohly, Athen. Mitt., 74, 1959, 54, Fig. 7. *Cf. pp. 58, 63.*

4 – Funerary statue of a youth. Marble. 630–620 B.C. Height 6 ft. 5 in. New York, Metropolitan Museum. G. M. A. Richter, Metropol. Museum Studies, V, 20ff. *Cf. pp. 65, 68, 130.*

5 – Seated statue, votive offering of Aeakes. Marble. From the town of Samos. About 530 B.C. Height 5 ft. Pythagoreion Museum. E. Buschor, Altsamische Standbilder, Fig. 141. *Cf. p. 132.*

6/7 – Bronze helmet from the sanctuary of Zeus at Olympia, with nails round the edge and inlaid spirals. Silver. About 560–550 B.C. Height 9 in. Olympia Museum. E. Kunze, VII. Olympia-Bericht, 84, no. 39, Plates 52 and 53. *Cf. p. 112.*

8 – Armour and helmet from a Geometric grave at Argos. Bronze. 8th century B.C. Height of armour 19 in.; height of helmet 18½ in. Argos, Archaeological Museum. Bull. Corr. Hell. 81, 1957, 322ff., Plates I–IV. *Cf. p. 28.*

9 – Breastplate from the sanctuary of Zeus at Olympia. Bronze. About 540 B.C. Olympia Museum. Arch. Deltion, 17, 1961/2, II, Plate 134a. *Cf. p. 112.*

10 – Early Attic loutrophoros. About 690 B.C. Height 32 in. Paris, Louvre. Arias-Hirmer-Shefton, History of Greek Vase-Painting, Plate II. *Cf. p. 181.*

11 – Early Attic sepulchral amphora from Eleusis. First half of 7th century B.C. Height 4 ft. 8 in. Eleusis Museum (cf. Plate on p. 41). G. E. Mylonas, Protoattikos Amphorevs tes Elevsinos, Athens, 1957. Arias-Hirmer-Shefton, History of Greek Vase-Painting, Figs. 12, 13. *Cf. pp. 38, 181.*

12 – Lakonian volute krater. Second quarter of 6th century B.C. Height 15 in. Rome, Villa Giulia. P. Mingazzini, Vasi della Collezione Castellani, no. 423, Plate 42. *Cf. p. 105.*

13 – Head of Chelidon: metope from Thermon (cf. Plate on p. 78). H. Kähler, Das griechische Metopenbild, Plate 19. *Cf. pp. 78 f.*

14 – Head of a kore, from the Acropolis. Marble. About 510 B.C. Height 6 in. Athens, Acropolis Museum, 643. H. Payne, Archaic Marble Sculpture from the Acropolis, 37ff., Plates 70, 71. *Cf. p. 185.*

15 – Lakonian cup: picture on the inside. About 550 B.C. Diameter 7 in. London, British Museum, B 1. *Cf. pp. 38, 105.*

16 – East Greek amphora in the Fikellura style. About 550–530 B.C. Height 12 in. Altenburg, Staatl. Lindenau-Museum. Corpus Vasorum Antiquorum Deutschland 17, Altenburg 1, Plates 10–12. *Cf. pp. 157, 161 f.*

17 – Peplos kore from the Acropolis. Marble. About 530 B.C. Height 3 ft. 11 in. Athens, Acropolis Museum, 679. Schrader-Langlotz, Die Archaischen Marmorbildwerke von der Akropolis, 45, no. 4, Plates 3–8. *Cf. pp. 165, 185.*

18 – The Gorgon Medusa with her children Pegasos and Chrysaor between two panthers. Central group from the pediment of the temple of Artemis in Corcyra. Calcareous sandstone. About 580 B.C. Height of the Gorgon 9 ft. 3 in. Corcyra Museum. G. Rodenwaldt, Korkyra: die Bildwerke des Artemistempels, Berlin, 1939. *Cf. pp. 85 f., 149, 195.*

19 – Two lions slaughtering an ox. High relief on a late Archaic pediment. Marble. Combination of casts of the separated halves in New York, Metropolitan Museum, and Athens, National Museum. Towards 500 B.C. Height 24½ in. G. M. A. Richter, Catalogue of Greek Sculpture in the Metropolitan Museum of Art, Plate X, 7. *Cf. p. 196.*

We obtained the original photograph for Plate 1 from the National Museum in Stockholm; the other photographs were kindly put at our disposal by the Museum for Casts of Classical Statues, Munich.

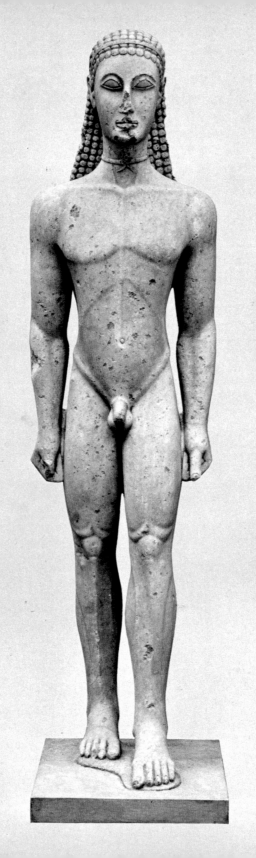

6

7

8

10

11

12

13

14

15

16

NOTES ON THE TEXT

PAGE 4   Any survey of the Archaic art of Greece is indebted to the monographs of Humfry Payne above all else for the firm chronological framework. But in these monographs he also showed how the methodical treatment of one single kind of monument illuminates at the same time other phenomena parallel in space or time, and indeed even earlier or later aspects of the history of art. To this extent one can say that the work of this man who died at the age of thirty-four must form the foundation for a fresh approach to the art of Archaic Greece; especially because few have recognized as clearly as he the specific problems of Archaic art and still fewer have been capable of saying anything appropriate about it, of helping to understand it or of contributing to the solution of its problems. Of his writings I should like to mention in particular:

Early Greek Vases from Knossos, in BSA, 29, 1927/28, 224.

Cycladic Vase-Painting of the Seventh Century, in JHS, 46, 1926, 203.

Protokorinthische Vasenmalerei, Berlin, 1933.

Necrocorinthia, Oxford, 1931.

Perachora, I: Oxford, 1940; II: Oxford, 1962.

Archaeology in Greece, 1931–32, in JHS, 52, 1932, 236.

A Bronze Herakles in the Benaki Museum, Athens, in JHS, 54, 1934, 163.

Archaic Marble Sculpture from the Acropolis, London, 1936.

Biography of Payne:

D. Powell, The Traveller's Journey is Done, London, 1943.

PAGE 11   GENERAL LITERATURE:

F. Matz, Die geometrische und die früharchaische Form (Geschichte der griechischen Kunst, vol. I), Frankfurt-on-Main, 1950.

ARCHAIC SCULPTURE:

Ch. Picard, Manuel d'Archéologie grecque, I, Paris, 1935.

ARCHITECTURE:

W. B. Dinsmoor, The Architecture of Ancient Greece, London-New York-Toronto-Sydney, 1950.

G. Gruben, Die Tempel der Griechen, Munich, 1966.

PAGE 12   V. R. d'A. Desborough, Protogeometric Pottery, Oxford, 1952.

PAGE 14   K. Kübler, Kerameikos V, 1, Berlin, 1954.

N. Himmelmann-Wildschütz, 'Der Mäander auf geometrischen Gefässen', in Marburger Winckelmann-Progr., 1962, 10.

PAGE 16   G. Hafner, 'Eine submykenische Stierplastik', in Jahrb., 58, 1943, 183.

D. Ohly, 'Frühe Tonfiguren aus dem Heraion von Samos', I, in AM, 65, 1940, 57.

PAGE 17   H. Biesantz, Die thessalischen Grabreliefs, Mainz, 1965.

PAGE 21   H. Marwitz, 'Kreis und Figur in der attisch-geometrischen Vasenmalerei', in Jahrb., 74, 1959, 52.

H. Marwitz, 'Neue geometrische Tierbronzen', in Pantheon, 23, 1965, 359.

N. Himmelmann-Wildschütz, Bemerkungen zur geometrischen Plastik, Berlin, 1964.

K. Reinhardt, Die Ilias und ihr Dichter, Göttingen, 1961.

PAGE 22   J. M. Davison, Attic Geometric Workshops, New Haven, 1961.

PAGE 23   R. Hampe, Die Gleichnisse Homers und die Bildkunst seiner Zeit, Tübingen, 1952.

H. V. Herrmann, 'Werkstätten geometrischer Bronzeplastik', in Jahrb., 79, 1964, 17.

PAGE 24   P. Courbin, 'Argos: Nécropole et céramique', in BCH, 78, 1954, 180.

PAGE 27   P. Courbin, 'Une tombe d'Argos', in BCH, 81, 1957, 322.

PAGE 29   H. Drerup, 'Zum geometrischen Haus', in Marburger Winckelmann-Progr., 1962, 1.

E. Buschor, 'Frühe Bauten', in AM, 55, 1930, 1.

PAGE 31   D. Ohly, 'Die Göttin und ihre Basis', in AM, 68, 1953, 27.

PAGE 33   *H. Schleif*, 'Altarplatz im Heraion von Samos', in AM, 58, 1933, 157.

PAGE 35   *T. J. Dunbabin*, The Greeks and their Eastern Neighbours, London, 1957.

                T. J. Dunbabin, The Western Greeks, Oxford, 1948.

PAGE 36   *R. D. Barnett*, Catalogue of the Nimrud Ivories, London, 1962.

                E. Löwy, 'Typenwanderung', in ÖJh, 12, 1909, 243 and 14, 1911, 1.

                E. Homann-Wedeking, Anfänge der Grossplastik, Berlin, 1950.

PAGE 37   *P. Bocci*, Ricerche sulla ceramica cicladica, Rome, 1962.

                I. Ström, 'Some Groups of Cycladic Vase-Painting from the Seventh Century B.C.', in in Acta Archaeologica, 33, 1962, 221.

PAGE 38   *E. Mylonas*, 'Protoattikos Amphorevs tes Elevsinos', Athens, 1957.

PAGE 40   *E. Langlotz*, 'Eine eteokretische Sphinx', in Corolla Ludwig Curtius, Stuttgart, 1937.

                E. Kirsten, Das dorische Kreta, Würzburg, 1942.

                P. Demargne, La Crète dédalique: Etudes sur les origines d'une renaissance, Paris, 1947.

PAGE 42   *E. Kunze*, 'Anfänge der griechischen Plastik', in AM, 55, 1930, 141.

PAGE 44   Cf. the literature mentioned in connection with page 4.

                G. Rodenwaldt, 'Votivpinax aus Mykenai', in AM, 37, 1912, 129.

PAGE 45   *E. Douglas van Buren*, Greek Fictile Revetments in the Archaic Period, London, 1926.

PAGE 47   *H. Berve*, Die Tyrannis bei den Griechen, Munich, 1967.

                H. G. Plass, Die Tyrannis, 2nd ed., Leipzig, 1859.

PAGE 48   *W. v. Massow*, 'Die Kypseloslade', in AM, 41, 1916, 1.

                C. T. Seltman, Cambridge Ancient History, volume of Plates I, 274, Cambridge, 1927.

PAGE 50   *K. Schefold*, Classical Greece (ART OF THE WORLD series), Appx. Pl. 18 and Fig. 36, London, 1967.

PAGE 52   *M. Collignon*. 'La statuette d'Auxerre', in Monuments Piot, 20, 1913, 5.

                J. Marcadé, 'Notes sur trois sculptures archaiques récemment reconstituées à Délos', in BCH, 74, 1950, 181.

PAGE 55   *W. Schiering*, Werkstätten orientalisierender Keramik auf Rhodos, Berlin, 1954.

PAGE 56   *Ch. Clairmont*, Das Paris-Urteil in der antiken Kunst, Zurich, 1952.

PAGE 58   *E. Buschor*, Altsamische Standbilder, vol. IV, Berlin, 1960.

PAGE 61   *D. Ohly*, 'Zur Rekonstruktion des samischen Geräts mit dem Elfenbeinjüngling', in AM, 74, 1959, 48.

                H. Walter, Das griechische Heiligtum, Munich, 1965.

                E. Kunze, IV. (VII.) Bericht über die Ausgrabungen in Olympia, Berlin, 1944 (1961).

                G. Richter, Kouroi, 1st ed., New York, 1942; 2nd ed., London, 1960.

PAGE 63   *F. Nietzsche*, Die Philosophie im tragischen Zeitalter der Griechen, Manuscript of 1873, published posthumously.

PAGE 65   *G. v. Kaschnitz-Weinberg*, Formprobleme des Übergangs von der archaischen zur klassischen Kunst, Manuscript of 1948, published in Ausgewählte Schriften, vol. I, Berlin, 1965.

PAGE 68   *E. Buschor*, Frühgriechische Jünglinge, Munich, 1950.

PAGE 72   *E. Harrison*, 'Fragments of an Early Attic Kouros from the Athenian Agora', in Hesperia, 24, 1955, 290.

                E. Homann-Wedeking, 'Echtheitsargumente', in AA, 1963, 225.

PAGE 79   *Sp. Marinatos*, 'Le temple géométrique de Dréros', in BCH, 60, 1936, 214.

PAGE 82   *E. Buschor*, 'Ein Kopf vom Dipylon', in AM, 52, 1927, 205.

PAGE 84   *G. Rodenwaldt*, Korkyra II, Berlin, 1939.

PAGE 87   *E. Spartz*, Das Wappenbild des Herrn und der Herrin der Tiere in der minoisch-mykenischen und frühgriechischen Kunst, Diss., Munich, 1962.

                E. Dyggve et al., Das Heroon von Kalydon, Copenhagen, 1934.

PAGE 88   *H. Bengtson*, Griechische Geschichte, 2nd ed., Munich, 1960.

PAGE 93   *E. Buschor*, 'Altsamische Stifter', in Festschrift Bernhard Schweitzer: Beiträge zur klassischen Altertumswissenschaft, Stuttgart, 1954.

PAGE 98   *E. Langlotz*, Frühgriechische Bildhauerschulen, Nuremberg, 1927.

PAGE 99   Cf. the literature mentioned in connection with page 4.

PAGE 100   *W. H. Schuchhardt*, in H. Schrader, Die archaischen Marmorbildwerke der Akropolis, Frankfurt-on-Main, 1939.

PAGE 103   *Ch. Tsirivaku-Neumann*, 'Zum Meister der Peploskore', in AM, 79, 1964, 114.

PAGE 105   *A. Lane*, 'Lakonian Vase-Painting', in BSA, 34, 1933/34, 99.

PAGE 107   *J. D. Beazley*, The Development of Attic Black-Figure, Berkeley & Los Angeles, 1st ed., 1951, 2nd ed., 1964.

PAGE 113   *J. D. Beazley*, 'Potter and Painter in Ancient Athens', in Proceedings of the British Academy, vol. XXX.
     E. Kunze, Archaische Schildbänder (Olympische Forschungen, II), Berlin, 1950.

PAGE 115   *J. D. Beazley*, Attic Black-Figure, London, 1928.

PAGE 119   *A. v. Gerkan*, Der Poseidonaltar bei Kap Monodendri, Berlin, 1915.

PAGE 123   *H. Kähler*, Das griechische Metopenbild, Munich, 1949.

PAGE 125   Cf. the literature mentioned in connection with p. 84.

PAGE 126   *E. Buschor*, 'Altsamischer Bauschmuck', AM, 72, 1959, 1.

PAGE 136   *L. H. Jeffery*, The Local Scripts of Archaic Greece, Oxford, 1961. Translation based on W. Peek, Griechische Grabgedichte, Berlin, 1960.

PAGE 143   *R. Joffroy*, 'La tombe de Vix', in Monuments Piot, 48, 1954, 1.
     A. Rumpf, 'Krater lakonikos', in Festschrift Ernst Langlotz 'Charites', Bonn, 1957.
     E. Homann-Wedeking, 'Von spartanischer Art und Kunst', in Antike und Abendland, 7, 1958, 63.
     M. Gjödesen, 'Greek Bronzes: A Review Article', in AJA, 67, 1963, 333.
     U. Häfner, Das Kunstschaffen Lakoniens in archaischer Zeit, Diss., Münster (Westf.), 1965.

PAGE 145   The view presented here is partly based on oral information, for which I am indebted to Chr. Karousos.
     Chr. Karousos, Aristodikos, Stuttgart, 1961.

PAGE 147   *H. Diepolder*, 'Eine Neuerwerbung der Münchener Antikensammlungen', in Antike Kunst, 5, 1962, 76.
     S. Karousou, 'Sophilos', in AM, 62, 1937, 111.
     I. Scheibler, 'Olpen und Amphoren des Gorgomalers', in Jahrb., 76, 1961, 1.

PAGE 151   Sophokles, Ajax, vv. 657–63 and 815–23.

PAGE 152   *S. Karousou*, The Amasis Painter, translated by T. J. Dunbabin, Oxford, 1956.

PAGE 155   *W. Kraiker*, 'Eine Lekythos des Amasis im Kerameikos', in AM, 59, 1934, 19.

PAGE 158   *A. Rumpf*, Chalkidische Vasen, Berlin, 1927.

PAGE 161   *R. Cook*, 'Fikellura Pottery', in BSA, 34, 1933/34, 1.

PAGE 168   *A. Rumpf*, 'Endoios: ein Versuch', in Critica d'Arte, 3, 1948, 41.

PAGE 169   *P. de La Coste-Messelière*, 'Au musée de Delphes', Paris, 1936.
     E. Langlotz, Zeitbestimmung der strengrotfigurigen Vasenmalerei und der gleichzeitigen Plastik, Leipzig, 1920.

PAGE 174   *E. Lapalus*, Le fronton sculpté en Grèce, Paris, 1947.

PAGE 177   *F. Krauss*, Die Tempel von Paestum, I: Der Athenatempel, Berlin, 1959.

PAGE 180   *A. Bruhn*, Oltos and Early Red-Figure Vase-Painting, Copenhagen, 1943.

PAGE 184   *K. Schefold*, 'Kleisthenes', in Museum Helveticum, 3, 1946, 59.

PAGE 185   Cf. the literature mentioned in connection with page 4.

PAGE 188   *F. Hiller*, Untersuchungen zur Ornamentik der attischen Vasen des 5. und 4. Jahrhunderts v. Chr., Diss., Munich, 1955 (unpublished).

PAGE 190   *E. Löwy*, Der Beginn der rotfigurigen Vasenmalerei, Vienna, 1938.

PAGE 193   *W. F. Otto*, Dionysos, Frankfurt-on-Main, 1933.

ABBREVIATIONS USED IN THE NOTES

AA   = Archäologischer Anzeiger (Supplement to: Jahrbuch des Deutschen Archäologischen Instituts)
AJA   = American Journal of Archaeology
AM   = Mitteilungen des Deutschen Archäologischen Instituts, Athenische Abteilung
BCH   = Bulletin de Correspondance Hellénique
BSA   = Annual of the British School at Athens
Jahrb.   = Jahrbuch des Deutschen Archäologischen Instituts
JHS   = Journal of Hellenic Studies
ÖJh   = Jahreshefte des Österreichischen Archäologischen Instituts

GLOSSARY

abacus
Topmost member of a capital, leading on to the entablature. In the Doric order, a square, smooth covering slab; in the Ionic, adorned with a kymation.

alabastron
Small bag-shaped ointment-flask, named after the material from which it was originally made.

amphora or amphore, plur. amphorae
Storage vessel with two handles; with the so-called neck-amphora the neck meets the body at a sharp angle and the handles reach up vertically to the neck; with the ordinary amphora the neck merges directly into the shoulders and belly of the vase.

aryballos
Small, bulging oil-flask with one handle and a flattened mouth; more recent examples are mostly spherical.

cella
Nucleus of every temple: a rectangular structure of square stones for the cult statue.

chiton
Shirt-like garment of thin material, usually with relatively short sleeves which are normally buttoned, very seldom sewn; it can be worn with or without a belt and either alone or under another garment.

denticulation
Row of projecting 'beam ends' leading, in the Ionic order, from the architrave to the cornice and framed by kymatia.

echinus
In the Doric capital, the round 'cushion' between the shaft of the column and the abacus; in the Ionic capital, egg-and-tongue bolster between the volutes.

entasis
The perceptible yet not exaggerated convex curve in the outline of the column.

geison, plur. geisa
Cornice projecting sharply over the **entablature** of columns (horizontal geison) or enclosing a pediment (sloping geison).

kantharos, plur. kantharoi
Drinking vessel with two high-curving handles. Attribute of Dionysos.

komos
Procession of joyous drinkers or komasts.

kore, plur. korai
The Greek word for 'maiden'; modern term for Archaic statues of maidens in Dorian or Ionian dress.

kouros, plur kouroi
Greek for 'youth'; modern term for Archaic

statues of naked youths, whose more precise significance can often not be determined.

krater
Open vessel for mixing wine and water; these vases are divided into volute and column kraters according to the shape of the handles. A later type is known because of its general shape as a calyx krater.

kymation, plur. kymatia
Moulding with a curved cross-section (kyma = wave), mostly employed in architecture. The simplest kymation is a semicircular horizontal rod with no vertical divisions. The most commonly employed 'Ionic kymation' has vertical divisions, which make it into an 'egg-and-dart' or 'egg-and-tongue' moulding. In the 'Lesbian kymation' the leaves have pointed instead of rounded ends and an S-shaped cross-section.

Lapiths
A Greek race which lived in Thessaly; to it belonged the invulnerable Kaineus and also Peirithoos, the friend of Theseus. At Peirithoos' wedding there was a quarrel with the Centaurs, who had been invited as guests.

lekythos
Little ointment-bottle or bigger oil-jug used for pouring libations to the dead; frequently placed in graves.

lygos
A bush which if tended develops into a tree, with a blue blossom (botanical name: *agnus castus* = withy).

Maenads
Greek for 'raving women', women in doeskins and long robes belonging, together with the Satyrs, to the ecstatic retinue of Dionysos.

metopes
Slabs adorned with paintings or reliefs which alternated in the Doric entablature with the double-ridged triglyph slabs (metope and triglyph frieze).

opisthodomos
Room in a temple adjoining the rear wall of the cella, open on the west side or closed by a bronze grille, used as a treasury.

peplos
Sleeveless garment of thick woollen material; almost always worn with a belt and frequently with an 'overlap' reaching down almost to the belt. The peplos is usually fastened on the shoulders with pins; on the right-hand side of the body, where the two edges of the material meet, it can be sewn or just left open.

pinakes
Painted tablets of wood or clay deposited as votive gifts in sanctuaries.

poros
Amorphous limestone of not very high specific weight which can be worked relatively easily when it is freshly broken off.

Pygmies
Mythical dwarf people whose cornfields were visited every year by cranes.

Satyrs
Mythical forest-dwellers, also known as Sileni, in the retinue of Dionysos; depicted as fat snub-nosed men with the ears, tail, and sometimes also legs, of a horse.

sima, plur. simae
Upper, relief-adorned edge of the roof-cornice with gargoyles, made of the same material as the roof tiles (marble or terracotta).

stylobate
Topmost course of the foundations of a temple, on which the columns stand directly.

thiasos
Festive company of singers and dancers, especially the Dionysian revelling of Satyrs and Maenads.

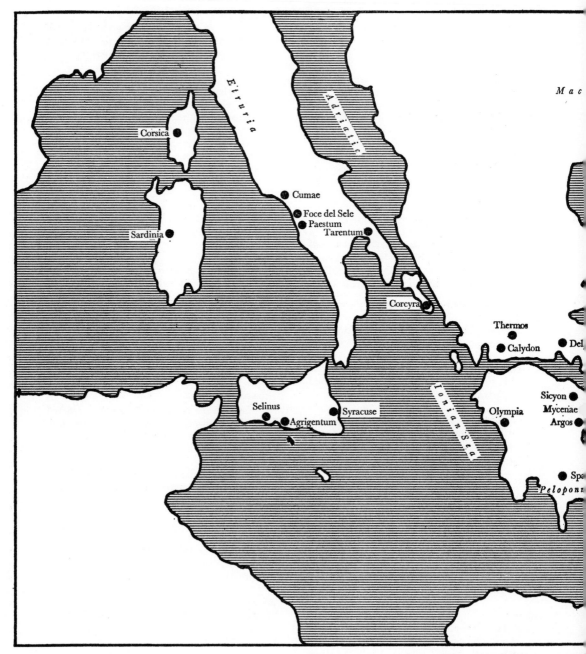

Corsica

Etruria

Adriatic

Mac

Cumae
Foce del Sele
Paestum
Tarentum

Sardinia

Corcyra

Thermos
Calydon
Del

Ionian Sea

Sicyon
Mycenae
Argos

Selinus
Agrigentum
Syracuse

Olympia

Spa
Peloponn

THE GREEK CITIE

INDEX

The numerals in italics refer to the plates and figures. The letter (G) denotes Glossary, the letters A.P. the Appendix of Plates.

abacus (G), 125f.
Achilles legend 110; Achilles and Ajax playing 152, 163, 165, *166;* Achilles and Briseis 180, 192; Achilles tending Patroklos *3,* 188
Acropolis: cf. Athens
Acropolis Museum: cf. Athens
Aeakes 132f., *A.P. 5*
Aëdon 77
Aegean Sea 36
Aegina: bronze-casting 138; hero 152
Aeolic: capital 126, *127;* Ionians 11
Aetolia, Aetolian 75, 88
Agora: cf. Athens
agriculture 22, 88, 90
Aischros 184f.
Ajax 151f., *153,* 158, 163, 165, *166*
akroterion 103, 127
Alexandros 56
Alkmeonidai 130, 174, 191
altar 32, 113, 119, *122*
Altenburg 161
Amasis 147, 152f., 163, 181, 183, 186; Dionysos and komasts 155, *159;* Dionysos and Maenads 155, *156,* 157f., 181
Amazons 175, 187
amber 60
Ambracian Gulf 49
Americans 61, 178
Ampharete 135f.
amphora (G), 25, 38, *39,* 40, *41, 153,* 161, 163f., *166,* 179, *189;* black-figure 69, *70;* funerary *13,* 13, 18, 22, 37, 181, 194, *A.P. 11;* neck-amphora 155, *156,* 157f., 161, 181, 183, *A.P. 16;* red-figure 180, 183f., 186
Anakreon 183
Anavyssos 24, 130, *131,* 133, 146
Anaximander 63f., 65
Anchippos 150
Andokides 184, 186
animal: pottery 195; statuette 23, 81f.; on pediment *88-9,* 196, *A.P. 19;* cf. frieze *and under individual species*
antae 171, 178
Antenor 146, 174
Antiope 175, 187

Aphrodite 56
Apollo 21, 36, 87; Ismenios 145; Philesios 143ff.; sculpture of 23, 145ff., *148,* 175; temple of, Corinth 119, 121, *123;* temple of, Delphi 172ff., *174, 176,* 177; Apollo Philesios, temple of, Didyma 143; temple of, Eretria 146, 175; temple of, Thermon *74, 75, 78,* 121
appliqués 138, 142
archaeology 178
Archaic: architectural reliefs 168f., 174; armour 112; art 62f., 65, 92f., 95, 104, 115, 130, 190; Athens 113, 191; Attic influence 88; bronze-casting 138ff.; grave stelai 103; inscription 136f.; korai 167; miniature art 137f.; mythological pictures 85; narrative pictures 87; politics 191f.; reliefs 133, 136, 193f.; religion 193f.; sculpture 24, 68, 71, 99, 130, 165f.; Solonian reforms 88; temples 117ff., 120, 175; vase-painting 105, 147ff.; wars 190; writing 136
Archaic, early 40, 81-129, 138, 160, *A.P. 1*
Archaic, late 28, 130-196, *A.P. 19*
archer 179f., *189*
Archilochos 15
architect 74; architecture 29, 33, 65, 74f., 82, 87, 91, 117, 121f., 126, 168, 177; cf. *also under names of individual elements*
architrave 119
Argolis 52, 75
Argos: art 25; artistic region 24; grave 28, *A.P. 8;* Heraion 30ff.; krater 28; vase-painting 25f.; Argives 151
Ariadne 110
Aristodikos 146
armour 28f., 112, *A.P. 8;* armourer 105
army 47, 56
arrow 143
Artemis 36, 53, *56,* 84; temple of 87, 98, 118f., *120,* 121, *A.P. 18*
aryballos (G), 113, 115, 147
Asia Minor 11, 36, 64, 119, 132; northern 128f.
Assyria 56
Atalanta 110
Athena 85, 151; Athena Polias 52; Athena

Promachos 45; Athena Pronaia *75;* temple of, on Acropolis 146, 175; temple of, Paestum 122, 177, *178, 179;* Hera and Athena 165, *168,* 169

Athens, Athenians 23, 136, 151, 165; Acropolis *44, 88-9, 92,* 92, 95, 97, 100f., 103, 145f., 149, 165, 171, 175, 177, 183, 196, *A.P. 14, 17;* Acropolis Museum 99; Agora 61, 72, 178; amphora 40, *41;* Archaic 113, 191; art 24, 36, 38; bronze-casting 138; citadel 91; Dipylon *13,* 72, *73,* 74f., 82f., 103, 130, 184; frieze 169; history and politics 23, 79, 183, 185, 190f.; Ionian influence in 146, 157; Kerameikos 61, 72, 98f., 101, 115, 155, 186; National Museum 61, 130, 133; necropolis and graves 98, 135, 184; Parthenon 52, 175; Peiraieus 69, *70,* 144ff., 181; potteries 19, 45, 105, 107, 165; sculpture *101,* 103, 122, 135; temple of Dionysos 194; trade 90

athlete   66, 103, 135

Attic, Attica 15, 23f., 36; agriculture 90; amphora 25, 37, 69, 71; art 91, 98, 135; epitaph 136; festivals 191; handle 141; head 88, 101; hero 111, 175; inscription *137;* kore statue 145; kouros statue 130, *131;* nobility 67, 133; sculptor 68, 94f., 99, 135, 168, 171, 174; sculpture *15,* 16, 44, 94, 97, 116, 133, 183, 185f.; social life 24, 88f.; tombstone *100;* vase-painter 40, 69, 112, 115, 161, 193; vase-painting 26, 44, 105f., 107, 115, 157, 161

Attic, Early 27, *A.P.10-1;* cf. Anavyssos, Athens, Little Masters, Solon

Automedon   110

Auxerre, Lady of   52, 53, *54*

Bacchic scene 155, 158; thiasos 161

battle scene   22, 55f., 110f., *111,* 113, 140f., 143, 149f., 165, *168,* 169

beaker   155

beast of prey   92

Beazley, J.   161

Belgrade   17

belt   18, 21, 65, 67, 95

Berlin: Pergamon Museum   81, 83, 141

bird 91, 105, 113, 140, 150; cf. *also under individual species*

Biton   83

Black Dipylon ware   24

black-figure amphora 69, 180f., *189;* drinking-

cup 141; painter 115; technique 45, 160f., 165, 183; ware 147, 150, 152

blossom motif   107, 137

boar   *108-9,* 110

Boeotia, Boeotian   24, 138

Boston, Fine Arts Museum   128

Boulogne-sur-Mer, Museum 151, *153,* 158, 181

bow   143, 145

bowl   105

box   48, 140

bracelet   141, 188

breastplate   28, *A.P. 9*

Briseis   180, 184, 186, *192*

bronze: alloy 17; armour *A.P. 8;* breastplate *A.P. 9;* engraving 40; -casting 23, 138f., 145; handle *112,* 140f.; helmet *A.P.6-7;* inscription 52; krater 38, 141, 143, *144;* plaque 40, 42, *43;* sculptor 143; sculpture 17, 19, *20,* 23, 42, 44, *44,* 61f., *64,* 65, 137, *139,* 140, 144ff., *146, 148*

Bronze Age: sculpture 17; temple 30

brooch   141

bud motif   107

bull   *15,* 55, 123f., 196

burial custom 14; scene 22

Cabinet des Médailles: cf. Paris

Calydon: boar hunt *108-9,* 110; head of sphinx *86,* 88, 98

calyx krater   178, *182*

capital   75, 103, 118f., 124, *125,* 126, *127-8,* 129

carpenter, carpentry   22, 126

caryatid   171, 178

cattle   23

cauldron: handle   140f., *142,* 149

cedar wood   48

cella (G), 30f., 117f., 171, 178; walls *32,* 33f.

Celts   141

Centaur   82, 110, *111,* 112, *139,* 140, 143

Chalcis 158; Chalcidians 163; artist 160; inscription 158; krater 160, *162;* pottery 90, 158; vase 158; vase-painter 160; vase-painting 158, 160

chariot 22, 56, 61, 141, 149f., 169, 175, 187; race *108-9,* 110, 112; charioteer 22f., 61, *64,* 65, 143, 150; Charioteer of Delphi 145

Châtillon-sur-Seine   38, 141

cheek-piece   112

Chelidon   76ff., *A.P. 13*

Cheramyes   94

Chigi Collection   *3,* 55, 58, *60,* 107

chiton   (G), 50, 52f., 95, 124, 155, 167
Chrysaor   85, *A.P. 18*
circle motif   136
citadel 91, 101; cf. Athens, Mycenae, Tiryns
cities   44, 64, 79, 177, 193
Classical: architecture 121; art 63, 175, 190,
    196
clay: drinking-cup 141; head 58; krater 38;
    implements 155; metopes 76, *78*, 82; oil-
    jar 81, *83*, 115; plate *154;* pyxis *18;*
    statuette 16, 23, 42, 137; vessel 12, 49,
    137f.
clothing 23, 28, 31, 53, 66, 93f., 97, 104, 115,
    133, 167, 179; cf. chiton, peplos
club   113
cock   71
coinage   89
colonies   44, 122, 138, 150, 177
colonnade   171
column 75, *75*, 117ff., 121, 124f., *125*, 136, 171,
    178; column krater 160; grave column
    125, 136, *137;* half-column 178
Corcyra 50; gravestone 124, *125;* reliefs of
    pediments 75, 82, 91f., 149, 175, 195f.,
    A.P. 18; temple of Artemis 119, 175,
    A.P. 18; sculpture 83, *84*
Corinth: architecture 47, *48*, 75f.; as art centre
    24, 36, 42; bronze-casting 23, 138; helmet
    169; history 47f., 49f.; influence of 88,
    98; inscription 48f.; jug 58, 107, 111,
    195f.; metope relief 122; pottery 82;
    sculptor 50; sculpture 45; temple of
    Apollo 119, 121, *123;* trade 47; vase-
    painter 69; vase-painting 44f., 55f., 84,
    115; writing 136; Corinthians 91, 163,
    183; cf. Kypselos, Protocorinthian
cow   97, *99*
crane   111, 113, 115, 147
crest   21
Crete, Cretans 36, 42; art 24; belt 65; clothing
    53; palace 37; plaque 40, *43;* pottery 12;
    sculpture 52; temple *77*, 79
Croesus: cf. Kroisos
cult: of the dead 33; of Apollo Philisios 143f.;
    of Demeter 24; of Hera 29, 30f., 52; cf.
    Orphic, procession, vegetation
cup 38, *106*, 155, 163, *164*, *A.P. 15;* cf. drink-
    ing-cup
Cyclades, Cycladic: amphora 38, *39*, 71, *A.P.
    1;* art region 24; culture 53; marble 72;
    religion 36; sculpture 23, 52, 68, 94, 97;
    cf. Delos

Cyclopes   11

Daidalos   71
dance   157, 161
Delos 36, 53; excavations at 61; sculpture 55,
    74; temple of Apollo 126; temple of
    Artemis 53, *56*
Delphi 48, 77; metope relief 122; oracle 169;
    sculpture 83; Siphnian Treasury 165,
    168f., *170*, *171-2;* temples 75; temple of
    Apollo 126, *174*, *176;* temple of Athena
    Pronaia *75;* cf. Charioteer
Demeter, cult of   24
demon 85, 87, 150; fire demon 91
diadem   141
Didyma: altar of Poseidon near 119; priest-
    kings 132; temple of Apollo Philesios 143
Diomedes   110
Dionysos 155, 161, 193f.; and komasts 155,
    159; and Maenads *156*, 157f., 163; Sea
    voyage of 163, *164*, 178; temple of, Athens
    194
Dioskouroi   101, 165
Dipylon: cf. Athens
discus-bearer   103, *104*
distych   14
dog   45, 56, 110, 113
dolphin   163
Doric 15, 30, 42, 160; architecture 29, 119,
    122; art 40; capital *125*, 125f.; echinus
    126; order 52, 74, 117, 124, 171, 178;
    temples 47, 50, 74f., 79, 118, 121; proto-
    Doric 52
dove   82
drachma   89
Dracon   88
Dreros   79
drinking 66, 157, 163; -cup 105f., 141, 147,
    160, 186f., 195; cf. kantharos, rhyton
duck   81f., 83, *83*, 115, 140f.

eagle   105
echinus   (G), 125f.
Egypt, Egyptian: art 19, 74; campaign against
    169
Eleusis: amphora 41, *A.P. 11;* graves 24
Endoios   168
engraving   40, 138
en rapport motif   12
entablature   125f., 178
entasis   (G), 121
Ephesos: excavations at 118; relief 118;

statuette 65, *67;* temple of Artemis 119, *120,* 121

epic poetry   116, 150, 184

Epiktetos the Elder   186

epitaph   136

Eretria: pediment 187; temple of Apollo 146, 175

Ergoteles   115

Ergotimos 113, 147; Calydonian boar hunt 107, *108-9*

Eteo-Cretan   40

Etruria   90

Euboea 89, 158, 175; cf. Apollo (temple of, at Eretria), Chalcis

Euphronios 184, 186ff.; Peleus abducts Thetis 186f., *195*

Europa   123, *124,* 124

Euthykartides   74

Euthymides   184, 187

Euxitheos   *192*

excavations   61, 95, 100, 112, 118, 177

Exekias 115, 147, 149, 152, 155, 157f., 163f., 165ff., 178ff., 183, 185f., 190; black-figure technique 150, 152; Achilles and Ajax playing 163ff., *166;* Ajax prepares to kill himself 151, *153,* 158, 181; Nymphs amid vine tendrils 178f., *182;* Scythian archer 179, *188;* Sea voyage of Dionysos 163, *164*

expressionism   40

fable   63

festival 30; cf. Panathenaic

Fikellura vase   161, *A.P. 16*

filigree   141

fire: cf. demon

fishing   22

Florence: Archaeological Museum   107

Foce del Sele   124

fortification 72; fortress 11, 85

France   61, 141

frieze: of temple A at Prinias 79; of temple of Hera 33; of Siphnian Treasury 165, 168f., *168, 170;* of Parthenon 52; on pottery 19, 45, 55ff., 58, *60,* 107, 110f., 113, 115, 143, 152, 155, 157, 161, 187

funeral, funerary pyre 22; cf. amphora, games, grave, necropolis, procession, relief, statue, vase

furniture   18, 140

games 165, *166,* 179, 186; funeral *108-9,* 110, 150

geison   (G) 87, 93, 116

Geneleos 93, *94,* 155; Ornithe 93, 95, *96,* 97, 133

Geometric 11-34; architecture 29f., 61; armour 28; art 15ff., 19, 25, 35f., 44, 63; ornamentation 19, 136f.; pottery 11f., 15, 24; religious background 21f.; sculpture 15f., 23, 62; 'silhouette style' 37; sociological background 21f.; stylization 194; themes 14; vase-painting 15, 25f., 29, 38, 105f., 147

Geometric, early 26; late *25,* 37f., 79, 181; cf. Protogeometric

Germany   61

Geryon   150

giant   40, 41, *168,* 169, *170*

gigantomachy   175

goat   56

god 21, 29, 45, 52, 110, 143, 155, 158, 163, 169, 195; goddess 30ff., 36, 53, 97, 169, 187; cf. *also under names of individual deities*

gold: cup 48, *49;* diadem 141; plate 141; sculpture 141

Gorgon   85, 87, 107, 115, 119, 147, 149, 175, 195f., *A.P. 18*

graves: furniture 24, 141; cf. amphora, column, funeral, necropolis, relief, statue

Hadrian, Emperor   183

Hageledas   146

hair: band 67f.; -style 53, 58, 68, 103, 132f., 135, 145

handle: amphora 158; cauldron 140, *142;* volute krater 141

hare   45

head   58, 71f., *73,* 82f., *86,* 88, 99, 101, *102* 103, 135, 186, *A.P. 13,14*

Hector   151, 152

hedgehog   82

Helen   101, 160

Hellenes 11; Hellenic festivals 30; hellenization 60, 118, 132

helmet   18, 21, 23, 28, 112, 158, 163, 169, *A.P. 6, 7, 8*

Hephaistos   23

Hera: cult of 29f., 52; relief 52f.; statue 30 61, *94,* 132; temples of 29, 129; temple of, Argos 30ff.; temple of, Olympia 117f., 121; temple of, near Paestum 124, 177; old temple of, Samos *30,* 30, 32, 61, 75,

79, 93, *96*, 97, 116; second temple of, Samos *32*, 33, 126; in vase-painting 56; Hera and Athena in battle with giants 168

Heraklea 49
Herakleitos 194
Herakles 91, 150
heraldic animal 56
Hermes 56; Hermes carrying a ram 143, *146*
hero 45, 105, 110f., 165, 175, 179, 195
Herodotus 118, 169
Hesiod 47
Hipparchos 130, 184
Hippias 130, 181, 183, 185, 191
Hittite statuette 17
Hofmannsthal, H. von 95
Homer 26, 40, 158; Homeric hero 195; verse 14
Hoplon 112
horse *18*, 23, 38, 61, 71, 99, 113, 140ff., 143, 150; race 38, 160, *162*; horseman 33, 56, 99f., *101*, 105, 107; cf. Pegasos
hound: cf. dog
hunting scene 22, *108-9*, 110

ibex 37
Ibykos 183
Iliad 11, 21, 150
implements 18, 65, 137, 155
India 59
inlay 60, *A.P. 6, 7*
inscription 23, 49, 52f., 67, 74, 93f., 101, 113, 118, 124f., 128, 130, 132, 136, *137*, 158, 160, 180, *184*, 184f., 187
Ionia 14f.; eastern 15, 94; Ionians 11
Ionic: architecture 119; art, artists 132, 157; black-figure vase 135; capital 118, 126, *128*, 129, 178; colony 138; column 178; costume 167; influence 58, 146, 157, 168; kymation 119, 127; language 11; order 33, 124, 171, 178, 183; philosophy 64; potter 160; pottery 157f.; sculpture 95, 97; temple 29, 79, 118, 121, 183; vase-painter 160; vase-painting 158, 161
Italy 145; central 17, 90; colonies in 177; southern 44, 122, 138, 194
Itys 77f., 87
ivory: carver 59; carving 58ff.; statue 58, 61, 65, *67*, 69, *A.P. 1, 2*

javelin 186
jug *57*, 58, *59-60*, 107, 111, 195f.; oil-jug 55, 155; water-jug 113
Julius II, Pope 55

Kaineus 140
Kambyses 169
Kanachos 144ff.
kantharoi (G), 115, 155
Kastalian spring 174
Kastor 165
Keos 183
Kerameikos: cf. Athens
Kleisthenes 184f., 190f.
Kleitias 112f., 116, 147, 149f., 152; Battle with Centaurs 107, 110, *111*; Calydonian boar hunt 107, *108-9*, 110
Kleobis 83
Klitias: cf. Kleitias
Klopedi *127*
komasts *159*, 161
kore (G), 95, *95*, 145, 165, 167, 171, 174, 183
Korone 187
kouros (G), 61ff., 65, 67, 75, 82f., 130, 133, 143
krater (G), *25*, 26, *27*, *28*, 38, 107, 110, *111*, 113, 141f., 143, *144*, *162*; cf. calyx krater, column krater, volute krater
Kroisos 118, 130, *131*, 133, 146
Kybele 169, *170*
Kylon 79
Kypselos of Corinth 48, *49*, 49

Lakonian cup 38, *106*, *A.P. 15*; krater 141, *A.P. 12*; potter 106; style 142; tile *48*; vase-painting 105, 107
Lapith (G), 112
leaf motif 106f., 126f., 137, 188
leather: belt 65
Leda 165
legend 11, 31, 45, 76, 85, 87, 110, 115, 149f.
lekythos (G), *159*
Leonardos 61
Lesbos *127*
Leto 36
Life of Apollonius of Tyana 59
limestone: capital *127*; column 75, *125*; metope *124*; pediment *88-9*, *92*, 92f., 99; relief 50, *51*, 53; sculpture 52, *54*, 83f., *84*; temple 30
lion 38, 40, 55, 83, *84*, 85, 169, *170*, 196, *A.P. 19*; hunt 56, 58, *60*
'Little Masters' 107, 115
London: British Museum 38, 105, 180, 183, *192*
lotus 58, 128, 137, 151
loutrophoros *A.P. 10*

Louvre: cf. Paris
lozenge motif 161
Lydia 118, 132
Lydos 115, 147f., 150, *154*
Lygdamis 193
lyre 61, *62*, 69

Maenads (G), 155, *156*, 157, 161, 163
magic 29, 163, 181
Magna Graecia 122, 142, 177
marble: fragments 65, 133, *134;* head *73*, 99,
    A.P. 14; inscription *137;* kore 165, *A.P.
    17;* relief *104*, 142, *187;* Siphnian Treas-
    ury 168f., *170;* sphinx 99, *100;* statue
    53, *56*, 72, 96f., *98-9*, *101*, *131*, *184*, *A.P.
    5*, *19;* stele *127;* temple 126
Marmaria 75
mask 85
meander motif 14, 19, 26, 136
Medusa 85, *A.P. 18*
Megara 48
megaron 29
Meixis 125
Meleager 110
Meno: cf. Plato
merchant 36
metals 167, 169; alloy 138; belt 65; head 58;
    vessel 137f.; cf. bronze, gold, silver
metope (G), 52, 75f., 78, 82, 87, 122f.,
    124, *A.P. 13*
Miletos 64, *122*
miniature art 137f., 150
Minoan: civilization 11; forms 40; palace 11,
    37
Minotaur 110
monarchy 22, 35
Monodendri, Cape 119, *122*
monster 150
mother worship 21
Munich: amphora 187; cup 178; krater 38
music 90; musicians 22, 191; cf. singers
Mycenean: architecture 29; belt 65; citadel
    11, 52; painting 45; relief 50, *51*, 52f., 122;
    late Mycenean *15;* post-Mycenean 12
myth 110, 160; mythical scene 40, 175;
    mythology 48, 55, 63, 76, 85, 87, 150f.,
    161, 163

narrative picture 87, 91
Natural History: cf. Pliny
naturalism 63
Nearchos 111, 113, *114*, 115, 146f., 149, 150f.

Near East 17, 35, 60, 65, 118
neck-amphora: cf. amphora
necklace 31
necropolis *13*, 72f., 98; cf. graves
Nessos 107
Nestor 11
New York 71f., 130, 133, 143; Metropolitan
    Museum 65, 67f., 113ff., *114*, *139*, 140, 147
Nexos: bronze-casting 138; excavation at 61;
    marble 126; kore 96, 98; sculpture 55,
    61, 99; cf. Nikandra
niche 117
Nietzsche, F. 63
Nikandra 53, *56*, 68
nobility 23, 35, 67, 79, 132f.
Noicattaro *112*
nymph 179f., *182*

Odysseus 40, *41*, 44
Odyssey *40*, 150
oil-flask 113, 115, 155; -jar *83;* vessel *114;*
    cf. jug
Oltos 180f.; Briseis 183f., 186, *192*
Olympia: games at 66; helmet 112; ode 47;
    sculpture 23, 61, *64*, 65; temple of Hera
    30, 117f., 121; temple of Zeus 87, 175,
    A.P. 6-7, *9;* votive gifts 48
Olympus 158
omphalos *49*
opisthodomos (G), 118
oracle: cf. Delphi
Orientalizing Age 35-80; amphora 69f., *70;*
    architecture 50f., 74ff.; art 44; ceramics
    37ff.; foreign influence 35f.; ivory carving
    58ff.; plaques 40, *43;* political back-
    ground 35, 47; sculpture 42ff., 50f., 53ff.
Ornithe 93, 95, *96*, 97, 133
Orphic cult 194
owl 82
ox *A.P. 19*

Paestum: temple of Athena 122, *178*, 178;
    temple of Hera near Paestum 124, 177
painting: on frieze 33; on metope 75; on
    sculpture 93, 135; on stele 45; on stucco
    45; cf. vase-painting, wall-painting
palace 11, 37, 110
palmette 58, 127, 129, 137, 151, 158, 188
palm-tree 151, 158
Panathenaic festival 91, 184, 191
panther 85, *A.P. 18*
Paris, Judgement of 56, 160

Paris: Cabinet des Médailles 157; Louvre *43*, 44, *46*, 49, 52f., *54*, 99, *102*, 158, 181
Parthenon: cf. Athens
partridge 82
Patroklos *108-9*, 110, 112, 188
Pausanias 21, 71, 117f.
Payne, H. 99, 103, 185, 209
pearl ornament 48
pediment 45, 47, 75, 82, 84f., 87, *88-9*, 91f., *92*, 98f., 116, 119, 146, 168, 174f., 187, *A.P. 18, 19*
Pegasos 85, *A.P. 18*
Peiraieus: cf. Athens
Peirithoos 111
Peisistratos, Peisistratids 99ff., 103f. 130, 146, 165, 175, 183, 184f., 191
Peleus 110, 112, 187f., *195*
Peloponnese 23, 36, 42, 56, 79, 98, 133, 138, 140, 146; north-eastern 50, 82, 143, 145
peplos (G), *A.P. 17*
Perachora: temple 77
perfume flask *46*, 49f.
Pergamon Museum: cf. Berlin
Periclean age 33, 191
peristyle 75
Perseus 115
Persia, Persians 183; Persian Wars 190, 193; cf. Kambyses
Pheidias 193
Philadelphia: Museum 179
philosopher 62f., 65, 194; philosophy 35; cf. *also under names of individual philosophers*
Philostratos 59
Phocis 77
Phoenicians 60
Phrasikleia 136, *137*, 185
Phrygians 60
phylai 191
pinakes (G), 115
Pindar 193
plaque 40, 42, *43;* cf. pinakes
plate 147f., 149, *154*
Plato 62f., 65; *Meno* 71
Pliny: *Natural History* 143
Plutarch 11
poet, tragic 78; lyric 183; poetry 14, 181
Polydeukes 165
Polykleitos 147, 193
Polykrates 103, 132, 183f., 193
Polyphemos: Odysseus blinds Polyphemos 40, *41*, 181
pomegranate motif 106f.

portraiture 100f., 193
Poseidon 119
potter 11, 19, 42, 69, 82, 105, 107, 115, 146f., 151, 188, 192; cf. *also under names of individual potters;* potter's wheel 12, 16; pottery 23, 45, 91
Praxiteles 158
priest-king 132
prince 110f.; princess 141
Prinias, temple A 77, 79
procession: cult 33; funeral 22, 150; god 110; horse, horseman 56, 143; komos 161
Protocorinthian *3, 46, 59, 60*, 82, *83*
Protogeometric *17*, 24
Pygmies (G), 111, 113, 115, 147
Pythagoras 194
pyxis *18*

ram 143, *146*
Rampin: Collection 99; head 99, 101, 103; Master 101f.
red-figure style 106, 147, 165, 179f., 184, 186
relief 44f., 50, *51*, 52f., 75, 79, 84f., 87, 103, 111, 116, 118f., 122f., 128, 136, 138, 140ff., *144*, 168f., 175, 186, *A.P. 19;* funerary 103, *104*, 133f., 135f., *187*
religion 11, 14, 21f., 29, 36, 87, 116, 193; cf. cult, Delos, god, priest-king
Renaissance 55
Rhodes 15, 55, 160
rhyton 16
ring 141
rites, sacrificial 32
Rodenwaldt, G. 125
Roman: army 28, 47; period 143, 145, 183
roof 31, 33, 45, 47, *48*, 75, 78f., 88, 116, 126f.

sacrifice 97, *99*
Samos 33; bronze-casting 138; capital 129; clothing 53; head 58; history 193; inscription *184*, 184f.; lyre 61, *62*, 69; sculptor 136; sculpture 58, 93f., 99, 132f., 184; vase-painting 160; cf. Hera
sandstone *A.P. 18*
Satyr (G), 155
scroll 161
sculptors 68f., 116, 136, 184f.; Argive 83; Attic 95, 99, 174; Corinthian 50; Ionian 97; Naxian 97; Peloponnesian 146; Samian 94, 97; cf. *also under names of individual sculptors*
sculpture 29, 61ff., 65, 74, 87, 91, 97, 167, 174,

177, 185; large-scale 15f., 42f., 53f., 61, 65, 82, 84, 105; small-scale 15f., 42f., *46*, 49, 82; cf. head, kore, kouros, relief, statue(tte), votive
Scythian   179f., *189*
seal ring   45
Selinus   52, 123, *124*
shield 28, 85, 112, 158, 163, 169; goddess 45; handle *112*
ship   163, 178
Sicily 44, 138, 177; Sicilian *48*, 52
Sicyon   48, 143, 145
signature of artist   72, 74, *108-9*, 113, *114*, 155, 157, 187f.
Sileni   161
silver: cup 141; nails 112
Simonides of Keos   183
singers   22
Siphnos, Siphnians 169; Siphnian Treasury (Delphi) 165, *168*, 168f., *170*, 171, *172*, 178
siren   82, 150
slavery   89
smith   21ff.
snake   85, 91
Solon, reforms of   88ff., 91, 191
Sophilos   112f., 149f., 161
Sophokles   151f., 193
Sosias   188
Sparta: Athena, patroness of Sparta 45; bronze-casting 23, 138; history 35, 89; pottery 106; relief 101; vase-painting 28
spear   28, 33, 110, 165, 188
sphinx   56, 82f., *86*, 88, 98f., *100*, 101
spiral motif   26
sport 22, 90, 104, 193; cf. athlete
'spread-out style'   44
stag   *17*, 37f., 40, 143, *A.P. 1*
statue 29ff., 33, 48, 55, 61, 66, 69, 72f., 81ff., *93*, *94*, *96*, *99*, 132f., 137, 144, 146, 175, *A.P. 2*, *3*, *5*; funerary 66f., 130, *131*, *184*, 186, *A.P. 4*; statuette 16ff., 19f., *20*, 21, 23, 28, *44*, 44, 48, 58, 61f., *64*, 65, *67*, 137, 141; cf. kore, kouros, votive
stele   103f., *127*, *128*, 128, 135
Stockholm   38
stone: architecture 33f., 75, 118f., 125; pediment 82; sculpture 61
stucco   45
stylization   19, 22, 28, 37, 63, 69, 84, 123f., 126, 133, 194
stylobate   (G), 75, 121
swan   140, *142*

Switzerland   177
sword   28, 151
symbol 14, 32; symbolism 21, 87, *124*, 151
symposium   161
Syracuse   47, 50, 138
Syria, Syrians   17, 60

Tarentum: bronze-casting   138, 142
temple 18, 29, 33, 47, 74, 81, 91, 111, 116, 171; cf. Apollo, Artemis, Athena, Dionysos, Hera, Perachora, Zeus
templum in antis   29
tendril motif   137
Tereus   77
terracotta: head of sphinx *86*, 88, 98; model of temple *77*; sculpture *15-17*
Thales   63f., 65
Thebes: flask   42, 44, *46*, 49, 115
Theodoros   118
Thermon: influence of Corinth on 88; metope *A.P. 13*; temple of Apollo 74ff., *78*, 79, 82, 87, 123
Theron   75
Theseus, King   11, 22, 110f., 175, 187
Thessaly: as art centre 24; battle scene 140; bronze-casting 23; prince 111; statuette 28
Thetis 110; Peleus abducts Thetis 187f., *195*
thiasos   (G), 161
tile   45, *48*
Tiryns, citadel of   30
Tleson   115
tomb *84*, 84, 105, 141; tombstone *100*
tools, household 22; cf. implements
trade   42, 47, 65, 89f., 150
treasury: cf. Siphnian
tree, sacred   32
triangle motif   136
Triton   91
Troilos   110
Troy 29, 151, 165, 179; Troad 152; Trojan 110, 160
tympanon   46f.
Tyndareus   165
Typhon   91, 93
tyrant 99, 105, 132, 181, 184; tyranny 47f., 79, 90, 103, 183, 193
Tyrrhenian amphora   161

vase *3*, 18, 22, 42, 44f., 55f., 58, 82, 126, 135, 140f., 151; funerary 12, 16, 18, 22f.; cf. *also under individual shapes*
vase-painter 19, 37, 42, 56, 69, 111ff., 115,

136, 147, 150f., *154*, 155, 160f., 180f., 184, 193; cf. 'Little Masters' *and under names of individual painters*

vase-painting 14f., 22f., 26, 28, 37, 42, 44f., 66, 71, 74, 84f., 91, 105ff., 112f., 115, 147, 149, 158, 161, 178, 184, 186, 188; cf. black-figure, Fikellura, red-figure

Vatican   165

vegetation cult   21

Veii   *59*

vessel 11, 24, 138; mixing-vessel 178

vine   *182*

Vix   141, 143, *144*

volute 105f., 125, 126f., 129, 137; volute krater *108-9, A.P. 12*

votive: offering 48f., 53, *56*, 79, 101, 126, 140; statue 23, 68, *96*, 103

vulture   105

wall 75, 116f.; -painting 33

warrior 29; on amphora 150, 180; on cup 188

weapon   21, 28, 112, 140, 158, 165, 179

weights and measures   89

wind   91

wine   160

wood: architecture 75f., 118, 125; -carver 22; sculpture 30, 61, 145

wrestling   91, 186

writing 136, 185; cf. inscription, signature

Würzburg   38, 160

Xenvares   124f., *125*, 136

Zeus 21, 169; on metope 52; on pediment 91; statue 48; temple of 87, 175, 183, *A.P. 6-7, 9*

zigzag band motif   26, 136

Zoilos   184